Apology to a Whale:

Words to Mend a World

Other works by Cecile Pineda:

Fiction:

Face

Frieze

The Love Queen of the Amazon

Bardo99: A Mononovel

Redoubt: A Mononovel

Nonfiction:

Devil's Tango: How I Learned the Fukushima Step by Step

Memoir:

Fishlight: A Dream of Childhood

Apology to a Whale:

Words to Mend a World

Cecile Pineda

San Antonio, Texas
2015

Cover photograph © 2013 by Bryant Austin, first appeared in *Orion Magazine*, Sept./Oct. 2013. Used by permission of the photographer. Figures 1 and 3 based on charts included in *The Horse, the Wheel and Language* by David Anthony (Princeton University Press, 2007). Figure 2 based on a chart included in *Before the Dawn*, by Nicholas Wade (Penguin, 2006). Used by permission.

ISBN: 978-1-60940-440-6 (paperback original)

E-books:
ePub: 978-1-60940-441-3
Mobipocket/Kindle: 978-1-60940-442-0
Library PDF: 978-1-60940-443-7

Wings Press
627 E. Guenther
San Antonio, Texas 78210
Phone/fax: (210) 271-7805
On-line catalogue and ordering:
www.wingspress.com

Wings Press books are distributed to the trade by
Independent Publishers Group
www.ipgbook.com

Cataloging In Publication:

Pineda, Cecile.
Apology to a whale : words to mend a world / Cecile Pineda.
xii, 210 pages
ISBN 978-1-60940-440-6 (paperback) -- ISBN 978-1-60940-441-3 (e-pub ebook) -- ISBN 978-1-60940-442-0 (mobipocket/kindle ebook)
1. Human ecology--Philosophy. 2. Ecolinguistics--Philosophy. 3. Environmentalism--Philosophy. I. Title.
GF21.P545 2015
304.201--dc23
                                          2015005048

CONTENTS

III. TWISTS IN THE ROAD

IV. LANGUAGE AS MIRROR

V. ON THE CONNECTEDNESS OF THINGS

VI. OUTLIVING CIVILIZATION

In memory of Barbara George,
friend, warrior, committed lifetime activist

We were in the water off Baja California in a very tiny little boat. A whale approached, an animal three times the length of our little boat. I became very friendly with this whale. When she allowed me actually to stroke her very tender skin, I noticed her tail flukes trembling with pleasure.

—Sebastiao Salgado,
in director Wim Wenders' "Salt of the Earth"

INTRODUCTION

The need to apologize to a whale—and to all living things—for the destruction mankind has wrought on our fragile planet is long overdue—but not many writers can claim to have been prompted by a whale, or the mis-appearance of a whale, because what I took at first to be a whale turned out to have been an enormous piece of debris ice, the detritus of a glacier calving episode. But for that piece of ice, this book may never have been written.

Ours is a global, technological civilization, but its wellsprings are rooted in Western, European thought. What is it about those whose work derives from a world view that guarantees the destruction of a planet where not only others, but they, too, make their home? Did humans lose something essential to their survival before we became human (if indeed we have become entirely human)? When Enrico Fermi split the atom in 1934 did he break the world apart?

Already as a child, the question of how people could do bad things in the world troubled me. When I asked my father, he explained my question had to do with what he called the "problem of evil." The problem went like this: "If God is all good, and all powerful, how can there be evil in the world?" Although my father was of a philosophical bent, and seldom imagined himself wrong, I discovered that God has little to do with the nuclear destruction of the planet, global warming, the Industrial Revolution, or for that matter, the language you happen to speak.

Apology to a Whale first examines the question: What did humankind lose with the discovery of speech and the use of language? The question seems relevant because plants and animals, creatures some refer to as "dumb," have managed to live sustainably for millennia, suggesting to me that, far back in the dawning of our primate origins, their intelligence may also have been part of our prehuman makeup.

Midway in the writing, the refinement of that first question led to an interrogation of the actual language complex spoken by the West, and of its role as vehicle of White European culture.

Some may wonder why I have chosen to limit my field of inquiry strictly to White, European history. I do so for the simple reason that its ultimate articulation is reflected in the overarching power arrangements—economic, geopolitical, and technological—that are destroying our present world. (See Jon Queally's "That Was Easy" in *Common Dreams*, 1.17.15.) I do not include the depredations of other peoples: the Mongols, the Aztecs, and others whose histories, just like those of the West, have had their points of origin and decline. Nor do I include other ethnicities whose languages are also derived from Proto-Indo-European. My concern as a product of Western Civilization and as a child of the New World rests exclusively with that of White European civilization as the *technologically dominant civilization of our time.*

With *Apology to a Whale,* I have spread out the map of what I consider characteristic of the present world's power relations: its "exceptionalist" hubris; its thieving resource wars; its chauvinism; its criminalization of poverty, of sickness, of blackness, of brownness, of redness, of female fecundity, of children, and of animals. I have tried to suggest how our present mode of existence is not only violent but deeply unscientific, that is, contrary to science's latest findings about the deep and eternal connectedness of all living things. I have limned the portrait of a civilization corroded by its own ruthlessness, and traced the origins of that ruthlessness to a linguistic cataclysm that occurred more than 6,500 years ago.

It is a civilization organized as a politico-economic system in which aggregates of capital fund multinational corporations claiming the power of speech, and whose agendas are represented by governments which, in the interests of their resource wars, represent the voice of people less and less. To dismiss its depredations in terms of greed is all too simple. Resorting to such tautology at best offers an ahistoric, apolitical explanation for the pornography of a global civilization determined to rape and mutilate the Earth, which gives us life, and sell her to the highest bidder.

Berkeley, California
March 11, 2014, the third anniversary of the
three-reactor meltdown at Fukushima-Daiichi, Japan

I.

THE THING WITHOUT A NAME

We are at the crucial moment in the commission of a crime. Our hand is on the knife, the knife is at the victim's throat. We are trained to kill. We are trained to turn the Earth to account, to use it, market it, make money off it. To take it for granted. Logically, we will never be able to reverse this part of our culture in enough time to stop that knife in our hand. But that is the task at hand—to cease this act of violence.

—Charles Bowden: *The Sonoran Desert*

1. "We who are about to die salute you."

*—cry of the Roman Empire's captives who
were forced to duel to the death*

In the great coliseum that is our planet, the dissolving glaciers are metaphor and reality, both at once, of our crumbling world. We watch the ice, like Civil War soldiers, lining up in ranks, facing an enemy lined up in ranks thousands of miles away. The command goes out:

FIRE!

and the first rank falls, mowed down by the opposition's bullets.

FIRE!

We watch the first rank fall, pulling the second rank behind it. Tor by tor, stalactite by stalactite, they tip, they fall, they rush headlong into the sea.

FIRE!

We hear the extra-arctic fire of car exhausts, of cars whose owners are driving around the block looking for a parking space, who leave their motors idling. Of coal-burning and oil-burning plants producing steam to drive the turbines that run the lights of cities so bright at night they can be seen glowing from space like poison fungi in the dark. You can even tell from space where the industrial countries lie: they glow the brightest, leaving the "developing" world in darkness.

Since 1765, the year that marks the first thunder of Watt's steam engine, you watch striations of soot pile up, zebra striping the blue of ice. Ice tilting crazily like layers of an onion, upthrust like geological strata, Earth's crumbling bulwark against the depredations of man—man's factories, man's cars, man's wanting to have more, more comfort, more to burn up, more to fill insatiable needs.

FIRE!

The ice won't go silent. In the frozen north comes the Great Thawing. *Boom* goes the third rank, boom of avalanche that growls too late. The ice has sounded its warning, but in New Orleans in 2005 no one can hear it. *Boom.* In 2011, in New England, no one can hear it. *Boom.* In 2012, in Staten Island, in Rockaway, on the shores of New Jersey, no one can hear it. They will drive. They will keep the lights on. They will drill for oil. They will frack for gas.

BOOM!

In Mindanao, under the cyclone's torrent, no one can hear it. Five thousand people drown. In Doha, the Climate Negotiators can't hear it.

Boom. This is the sound of the ice, the infrasonic rumble as it begins to fracture. Listen. Listen now. The rumble of the deep. Listen. Here it comes, gathering speed. Can you hear it? Can you feel the ground move beneath your feet? Here it comes, opening its jaws. This moment, when the rumbling gathers speed. Louder. It gets louder now. Yet louder. Can you hear…?

But no. You are in your soundproofed halls of power. You are meeting in Doha, capital of the richest per capita nation in the world, whose every citizen receives an annual subsidy from the oil you extract, oil that will be transported in pipes, in ships, belching smoke from their stacks, to plants where it will burn to make more light. So the earth can be seen from space, so the efflorescence of its light can delineate the littorals of its most developed countries, of its cities bathed in street light so bright they can be seen at night from outer space, sending out its SOS: We are burning. We are on fire, the fire, which is warring with the ice.

You too, line up in rows, protected behind the names of your countries here in Doha where the hostess of this global gala has dropped your nation's names like place cards. You cannot hear it. Earphones block your ears as you take in the simultaneous translation in your country's language. You cannot hear it as you prepare to speak. You cannot hear it under the factory lights of the great hall in which you sit sowing deception and delay.

Boom. The oceans are rising. The fourth rank of ice goes toppling, smashing into the deep. *Boom.*

The night of space does not hear. And behind their place names, the delegates wrap their heads in their earphones, sitting beneath industrial lights whose power is generated by coal-burning, oil-burning furnaces that turn turbines that make the power that guarantees that they won't hear, so that they won't see the infinitely small moment of cinematic* time when, amidst the cascading ice sheets, a whale heaves its huge bulk into the light to fix us earthlings with its great accusing eye.

2. The Art of Apologizing

> *When the Indians all die, then God will let the water come down from the north. Everyone will drown. That is because the White people never cared for land or deer or bear.... The White people plow up the ground, pull up the trees, kill everything. The tree says, "Don't. I am sore. Don't hurt me...." The Indians never hurt anything, but the White people destroy all.... How can the spirit of the earth like the White man...? Everywhere the White man has touched, it is sore.*

> — Kate Luckie of the Wintu Nation

How do you apologize to a whale? What can you tell it that it may not already know: how the seas in which it migrates thousands of miles each year are becoming more acidified with each season that passes. How the waters turn warmer, displacing the

---

* "Chasing Ice," directed by Jeff Orlowski, National Geographic, 2012.

denizens of the temperate waters farther towards the melting ice-caps? How the bodies of the small fry in the northern waters gape with the same ugly blood bruises of radiation sickness that surface on the skins of people living in Japan? How the larger fish eat the small fry, concentrating radiation upward in the food chain? How do you explain how one species, and only one species on earth has insisted on dominion over all things, driving the dynamic of its planetary habitat to chaos and collapse? What do you say? Do you tell it why in its migrations it must avoid the sea of plastic detritus big as Texas spiraling slowly in a now lifeless sea once teaming with plankton, and all forms of life. Tell it to steer clear from the very depths to the place where water meets sky where it breeches for air between its hour-long dives? How would you explain—or justify—something impossible to justify?

Would you offer the Earth's gaping wounds, its carbon emitting smokestacks, its fracking sites, its radiation-contaminated grounds as consolation? Or the feeling of entitlement in the western world to drive exhaust-belching cars, to fly planes, to contaminate its rivers and streams, to clear cut its own lungs, the trees; to kill everything that moves? To wage perpetual war for wealth and aggrandizement, and because one nation can blackmail another with knowledge of its secret acts, to decimate its own species by the millions and to leave behind a poisoned Earth wherever its armies bivouac?

Would you begin to ask yourself—or explain—where in time your minor species started to go wrong? Was there such a moment? Why did it come about? Were there several such moments? How would you explain the imperviousness of the Princes of the Earth as they go about the business of business, insulated in their high-rise, air-conditioned boardrooms, and in the hallways of Empire where the deals are struck and where mountain-by-mountain, forest-by-forest, invasion-by-invasion, assassination-by-assassination, they condemn the Earth to die?

Today as I write, co-authors Mark Halperin and John Heilemann's book appears. Titled *Double Down: Game Change*, it chronicles the passage of the most recent U.S. presidential election, alleging that a recent winner of the Nobel Peace Prize, wanting to reassure his aides of his qualifications as 44th president of the United States, averred that he is really good at killing. Granted, killing is part of the U.S. president's job description, and has been since the days of Andrew Jackson of genocidal fame, and those who came both before and after him. The wealth of the United States, like that of empires the world over, has been wrested from its victims: slavery of its black population, genocide of its First Nations—and from whale slaughter.

Many consider *Moby-Dick*, with its theme of lust for revenge and obsessive urge to destroy, the quintessential American novel. Here is Melville:

> How comes it that we whalemen of America now outnumber all the rest of the banded whalemen of the world; sail a navy of upwards of seven hundred vessels; manned by eighteen thousand men; yearly consuming 4,000,000 of dollars; the ships worth, at the time of sailing, $20,000,000; and every year importing into our harbors a well reaped harvest of $7,000,000? How comes all this, if there be not something puissant in whaling...? If American and European men-of-war now peacefully ride in once savage harbors, let them fire salutes to the honor and glory of the whale-ship, which originally showed them the way, and first interpreted between them and the savages.

Would I explain that—justify that—to a whale? Could I imagine making excuses, knowing all the while that my species was hell-bent on starving it, evicting it from its habitat? Would I comfort it by telling it how its blubber was boiled down to light the night, as oil is taken from the darkness of the earth to make light?

What might be the whale's response—assuming I were intelligent enough to hear it?

3. Slaughter of the Innocents

*Sperm whales are not every day encountered: while you may...
you must kill all you can...and if you cannot kill them at once,
you must wing them, so that they can be afterwards killed at your
leisure. Hence it is, that at times like these the drugg* comes into
requisition...*

—Herman Melville in *Moby-Dick; or, The Whale*

Originally the American continents were home to giraffes, hippopotami, saber-toothed tigers, woolly mammoths, and giant bears. Much of the same species of megafauna existed on the European continent as well. Humans are thought first to have arrived from Siberia via a land bridge called Beringeria some 13,000 years ago. Yet within 3,500 years, with the exception of a few remaining herds of bison, all megafauna had vanished from the continent. Of the thirty million bison once inhabiting North America, only twenty-three were left after the 19th century slaughter. It is said of the Clovis culture (roughly 10,000 B.C.), that within 500 years of its arrival across the Bering land bridge, all the great megafauna of the North American continent had become extinct. Clovis is known for a new technological breakthrough: more efficient flint arrowheads. Yet for all their technological advancement, Clovis people hunted their food source to extinction. Who or what was this primate who set hunting before the need to take no more than what is needed to sustain life? Was his fear greater than his hunger?

By 1725, the gray whale was extinct on the American East Coast. It was the first extinction of whales to be perpetrated by Western man in North America.

In the Indian Ocean, bowhead whales, originally numbering in the hundreds of thousands, were hunted by Yankee whalers to near extinction, stopped only by the maritime treaty of 1946.

---

* large wooden block attached as a drag to a harpoon

Now some few thousand survive. With advances in winching, it became possible to pursue whale species whose bodies sank after death. Americans, acting on a tip from a Chinese pilot, discovered that gray whales congregated in the waters off Baja California. Within 30 years, the grays became commercially extinct. Bottlenose whales followed. When the grays recovered, they were hunted again. And crashed again.

In 2013, Wildlife "Services" killed 4.4 million animals, half of them native species. The total includes roughly 75,000 coyotes, 900 bobcats, 500 river otters, 3,700 foxes, 12,000 prairie dogs, 100 red tailed hawks, 400 black bears, and—minimally— 3 eagles (golden and bald). Almost every day my e-mail swells with another petition to "save the wolves" as yet another initiative proposes they be shot, usually from the height and might of a helicopter. Every year, almost everywhere in America, cougars are shot because they wander away from their meadowlands and wilderness to blunder into the ever-expanding wilderness of housing tracts. Every year, baby seals are clubbed to death as soon as the new crop of pups is born. Every year, Denmark and Japan see the ritual slaughter of thousands of dolphins until the sea foams red with blood. In Africa, large mammals are killed by poachers for their meat, for their hide, for their tusks and for their horns. In mid 2014, the National Resource Defense Council issued a signature appeal following the fourth mass-stranding death of beaked whales on Greek beaches following joint sonar-based U.S. naval exercises.

Every year sees the expansion of an economic war against the poor, where people in Third World countries are paid close to starvation wages in factories that tend to singe them at their Singers. In every country where Walmart expands or Monsanto sells its seeds, native farmers either commit suicide or cross the U.S. border illegally to forestall starvation—and face either death by exposure in the deserts of Sonora, or the cruelties of the U.S. de-migration "service," where, just like welfare occupants of single-occupancy hotels, they are farmed like poultry in detention centers, some of them government owned, some of them privately held, earning at least 75 dollars a day for the prison system to enrich itself.

And now, thanks to the perpetual—and profitable—wars of the New World Order, almost every year sees the initiation of a new—and improved—war, where people of color and their children, preferably with oil under their sands, are hunted with very expensive and increasingly complex weapons that reap fortunes for munitions makers and the government enablers who hold vast stock in their enterprise, while three trillion of Pentagon expense goes "unaccounted for"—especially now that all accounting records have been disappeared in the physics-defying bombing of the Pentagon by a plane flying so low it smashed into the ground floor file rooms but left the outside lawn unsinged.

Humanistic education may have deluded humans into expecting something other than a biologically deterministic view of life on earth. At the very least, we can say that when animals hunt they don't make use of take-home boxes, although, perhaps because their prey is penned, mountain lions and wolves preying on domesticated herds and flocks have been known to leave behind multiple kills after their nights of depredation.

Yet the question persists: is there call for another way? and if there is, what is it? We give lip service to the principles of mutuality, compassion, and of responsibility for caring for our most vulnerable. We presume to abjure the appalling cruelties of pogroms, witch burning, crucifixion or burning at the stake of whistleblowers and trouble makers, of drawing and quartering, of dismembering, and other rituals of human dissection. And yet, beneath a perilously thin veneer, we smile with blood-red teeth.

4. Extinct Skies

Poets and Latin Americans are said to be sky gazers. We are not of a practical bent so much as dreamers. We read the skies, but we are not prognosticators of weather as much as shapes. My own wonderment at seeing the changing light of day from the dull blue gray that presages the dawn to the rose of day's dawning promise, the horizon rimmed with daybreak, the birthing rays of sunlight erupting over the hills, the flattening of the light as the day advances, the decline of afternoon, the lengthening shadows of evening, the mystery of the gloaming; more than waves of sand in the desert, or the shimmer of light on waves of the sea, it is the endless saga of sky that I never tire of reading as if each day, light is born anew.

People buried in isolation prison units see only artificial light. More and more of the 7.2 billion of us now on Earth can no longer venture into the open air because it no longer supports life. In China's capital, the skies have become so occluded under a pall of poisoned air, thousands flock to giant outdoor TV screens to watch a virtual sunrise because they no longer have any hope of seeing the sun. Imagining never seeing the sky means never again being allowed to live.

Centuries ago, under the very skies I now inhabit, swarms of passenger pigeons darkened the horizon, their migrations thick as tornados sweeping across the horizon—billions of them in one flock, rare and wondrous as any Perseid shower—the stuff of awe for those who lived to see and write about them centuries ago.

And yes, where are these now, these thundering wings as millions passed overhead within a single day, darkening the sun; where is the dung that fell like flakes of snow from flocks, which as late as 1860 could topple strong trees with their weight as they feasted on their fruits? People wielding torches clubbed them by the hundreds as they roosted in the trees at night. Railroad telegraphs hummed with news of approaching flocks so trappers could more efficiently prepare their nets to kill them by the thousands. Of these millions on millions, not one has survived, not one. More than the drowning of polar bears in the arctic melt, more than the relentless war against whales and dolphins, I rage at this extinction. Never have I felt such fury to think that because of human wantonness I will never welcome their reach over the horizon, the murmuration of their wings darkening the sky from daybreak to sunset. The skies of my days are wiped clean. They stare back at me accusingly, a mirror of man's fecklessness.

5. A Natural History of More

Lao Tzu wandering through the country stopped to chat with a peasant lady. Lao Tzu had noticed a sign on his approach to the town: WARNING! MAN EATING TIGER AT LARGE! Lao Tzu asked the lady why are you still living here? The lady replied, because in all other towns the ruler is evil and has control of everything and everyone. Lao Tzu said, yes, an oppressive government and monopoly power should be feared more than a man eating tiger. After all, a tiger only can eat its fill but Multinational Corporations and governments have a bottomless pit that never fills.

—Source unknown

In animals such as the horse, the wolf, even the domesticated dog, the heel breaks the line of the hind quarters in a far more esthetic way than our vestigial lowest joint (our foot), because, unlike most animals, we do not walk any longer on our toes. Consider the awkwardness of our heels. We take for granted that our appendages are unlike those of most animals. We do not have hooves, or cleft feet. If we examine our hands, if we read what they tell us, not the fortune-teller's lines—they're best left to other prognostications—but the morphology, we have what are called fingers, called by a cognate word that is found in almost any language spoken on earth. Unlike animals with toes, our fingers do not operate in parallel. They operate thumb to hand in opposition.

Sometimes I contemplate the millions of years it took to journey from claws and toes, to be washed ashore at last in our own time with an appendage in the shape of our own hands. And yet, our history has stamped us and not just with fingerprints. It is said that cats can count to three, an assumption based on the observation that often nursing cats when moving their litters, carry the first three kittens by the scruff of their necks, but leave the other kits behind. We do not carry our offspring in our teeth. At most we may cut a darning thread by severing it. Our upright position may have spoiled the esthetics of our hindquarters, but coupled with our oppositional fingers, and walking on two feet, we can carry as no other animal can. (Although insects in relation to their own bodies manage to carry objects many times weightier and more massive.) And we tend to count in multiples of five.

Imagine now that ancestor of yours—and mine—who subsisted on what he or she could gather. No longer having to walk, as did other animals, on all fours; able to grasp roots, nuts and seeds for the taking; able to fashion a crude carrier of some kind to gather more. And a basket to carry even more. To pile up even more in a small bee-hive strongbox that would last the winter and keep rats and vermin out, to build a granary to store even more. To build a silo to amass even more. To corner the futures market to control even more. As the Scots like to say: "Many mickles make a muckle." And that in short is Chapter One. Without two feet and oppositional thumbs we might never have learned greed.

Seeds and nuts and roots have little defense. Trees and grasses cannot run away or hide. But protein can. And although ungulates can elaborate it from vegetation and vegetation only, the primate stomach began losing this ability millions of years ago. To eat protein we would have to kill. But without appropriate tools, we could only avail ourselves of stones. For our first taste of protein, we would look to the mega-carnivores who left behind their putrefying kills. Our stones would smash the bones; our teeth would crack the fragments to suck out the decomposing marrow. We would learn to shape the stone, to chip stone with stone. We would make flint spears and arrowheads, we would fasten them to shafts with thongs of leather, or wild grasses. We could aim from afar and reduce our chance of danger; we could learn to kill cooperatively. And when we discovered metal and how first to forge bronze, then iron, we would shape a sharper weapon to kill yet more efficiently.

With better cutting tools we could draw and quarter our kill for easier transport. At first we took only what we ate. But with spears, we could decimate whole continents of the huge beasts living there. We could kill anything that moved, including those of our own kind who claimed our territory. We could claim new territory. We could abduct a neighbor's women, we could burn his fields, and villages, we could amass more fields, more rivers and forests, more mountains and valleys, we could conquer whole regions, we could decimate whole populations, we could force them towards the sea or inland when we wanted or thought we needed to.* We would complete yet more chapters in the long history of human greed.

Like the rich who live in East Carroll, Louisiana, America's poorest parish, where while they pocket an average $611,000 in annual farm subsidies, they resent the $1,492 food stamp allocation of the poorest of the parish, what characterizes the acquisitive class is that they must always have More. They must have More because they fear their lives may sentence them to Less.

*6. Footnote: The Trail of History

From *The Education of Little Tree*

The government soldiers came and told [the Cherokee] to sign the paper. Told them the paper meant that the new white settlers would know where they could settle and where they would not take the land of the Cherokee. And after they had signed it, more government solders came with guns and long knives fixed on their guns. The soldiers said the paper had changed its words. The words now said that the Cherokee must give up his villages, his homes, and his mountains. He must go far toward the setting sun, where the government had other land for the Cherokee, land that the white man did not want.

Now the government soldiers came and ringed a big valley with their guns, and at night with their campfires. They put the Cherokee in the ring. They brought Cherokees in from other mountains and valleys, in bunches like cattle, and put them in the ring.

After a long time of this, when they had most of the Cherokees, they brought wagons and mules and told the Cherokees they could ride to the land of the setting sun. The

Cherokees had nothing left. But they would not ride, and so they saved something. You could not see it or wear it or eat it, but they saved something; and they would not ride. They walked.

Government soldiers rode before them, on each side of them, behind them. The Cherokee men walked and looked straight ahead and would not look down nor at the soldiers. Their women and children followed in their footsteps and would not look at the soldiers.

Far behind them, the empty wagons rattled and rumbled and served no use. The wagons could not steal the soul of the Cherokee. The land was stolen from him, his home; but the Cherokee would not let the wagons steal his soul. As they passed the villages of the white man, people lined the trail to watch them pass. At first they laughed at how foolish was the Cherokee to walk with the empty wagons rattling behind him. The Cherokee did not turn his head at their laughter, and soon there was no laughter.

And as the Cherokee walked farther from his mountains, he began to die. His soul did not die, nor did it weaken. It was the very young and the very old and sick.

At first the soldiers let them stop to bury their dead; but then, more died—by the hundreds—by the thousands. More than a third of them were to die on the Trail. The soldiers said they could only bury their dead every three days; for the soldiers wished to hurry and be finished with the Cherokee. The soldiers said the wagons would carry the dead, but the Cherokee would not put his dead in the wagons. He carried them. Walking.

The little boy carried his dead baby sister, and slept by her at night on the ground. He lifted her in his arms in the morning and carried her.

The husband carried his dead wife. The son carried his dead mother, his father. The mother carried her dead baby. They carried them in their arms. And walked. And they did not turn their heads to look at the soldiers, nor to look at the people who lined the sides of the trail to watch them pass. Some of the people cried, but the Cherokee would not cry. Not on the outside, for the Cherokee would not let them see his soul; as he would not ride in the wagons.

And so they called it the Trail of Tears. Not because the Cherokee cried; for he did not. They called it the Trail of

Tears for it sounds romantic and speaks of the sorrow of those who stood by the trail. A death march is not romantic.

You cannot write poetry about the death-stiffened baby in his mother's arms, staring at the jolting sky with eyes that will not close; while his mother walks.

You cannot sing songs of the father laying down the burden of his wife's corpse to lie by it through the night, and to rise and carry it again in the morning—and tell his oldest son to carry the body of his youngest. And do not look...nor speak...nor cry...nor remember the mountains.

—Forrest Carter

These words were first published as non-fiction in 1976 by a writer who signed himself Forrest Carter, but whose identity as Asa Carter was later unmasked by a number of journalists, among them a distant cousin. They wrote to discredit the author, a man whose shifting identities plagued him and threatened others around him throughout his life—and whose psychotic behaviors branded him a psychopath, a White supremacist, drunkard, wastrel and pathological liar—and, because the book was first published as non-fiction, suggested it be dismissed as a hoax. Later published by the University of New Mexico Press as fiction, it continues to sell in the millions of copies. But regardless of the failings of its author, *The Education of Little Tree* retells what American history soft-pedals as the Indian "removal," with the accuracy of truthfulness. No matter what his failings, the author describes what has come to be known as the "Trail of Tears," and provides a truthful account of genocide, and what victims of genocide such as Effie Oakes Flemming's grandmother must have felt. In a native oral history dated 1937, she quotes her: "Everybody who was able... had to walk, but if babies gave out [and] the parents could not carry them, the drivers of the wagons would just take them and swing them against a tree and knock their brains out."

Tears come in many forms. To date, the present administration will have deported some 2 million so-called "illegals," most of them indigenous people, tearing families apart, returning people, some of them brought to the United States in their infancy and who have known no other country, to a despoiled Mexico where, thanks to NAFTA, because U.S. corn undersells Mexican corn, subsistence farming is now no longer possible. Would we call this ethnic cleansing because we can't admit to genocide? Today as I write, Lori Wallach, director of Public Citizen's Global Trade Watch, speaking on "Democracy Now" about the extremely secret TransPacific Partnership, stated, "There are new rights to... to enter other countries and take natural resources, a right for mining, a right for oil, [for] gas, without approval...." Where are the tears?

7. Twelve Terrified Apostles

"Rapture of the deep" is not anything like a poetic disease. If humans stay down too long beneath the surface of the sea, when they rise back up too rapidly, the gases in the blood expand, leading to excruciating pain and often death. But the whale can stay down thousands of feet, sometimes for longer than an hour.

Most Americans have lost the art of listening. Immersed in the raptures of its profit-driven apparatus, enthralled by the myths, which pass for its history, seduced by the razzle-dazzle of celebrity, best-seller, and sexual display, American culture leaves little oxygen for authentic views to surface. When a colleague prints out his last-minute reminder about this year's Hiroshima-Nagasaki Livermore observances on August 6, leaving out any mention of either of the women speaking, I am surprised by my feelings of anger and disappointment. When I take him to task, he insists I must be egotistical. He points out that the keynote speaker is world-famous. *He's* the one people *really* come to hear.

On that early August day in a chill and sunless Livermore, site of Lawrence Livermore Labs, where $20,000,000 has just been allocated to develop the Long-Range Stand-Off Weapon, including a redesigned nuclear warhead and delivery vehicle, people stamp their feet to keep warm. Some folks ask me if maybe I shouldn't be in bed nursing what seems to be pneumonia, but I'm scheduled by the organizers to talk about the connections linking nuclear energy production with weapons of mass destruction. I have a few words ready:

> Last week, the BBC reported that, now the Government of Japan, the Tokyo Electric Power Company, and the Japanese Nuclear Regulatory Agency finally admit that trillions of gallons of radioactive water have been leaking daily into the Pacific since the explosions of 2011—not to mention the existence of three melted cores—they have declared Fukushima an emergency. The nuclear industry is in the hands of clowns, crooks and criminals. From its inception, it has been inextricably linked to nuclear war. As early as 1953, Monsanto's then-vice president, Dr. Charles Thomas, pointed out that nuclear plants could not be a profitable undertaking unless they provided bomb-grade plutonium to the atomic weapons industry. He advocated creating a dual purpose plutonium reactor, one which could produce plutonium for weapons, and electricity for commercial use.
>
> We, and all others of like mind, are the only ones standing between a corrupt industry, both its weapons and energy making cycles, and—ultimately—survival of life on this planet. Many of us are here today because we want to lend our efforts to making nuclear war obsolete. Would it trouble you to know that we are engaged in a long-existing nuclear war right NOW? Without nuclear plants there can be no nuclear weapons and this is true of so-called "depleted" uranium as well. Depleted uranium, whitewashed by the industry as DU, is the by-product of the fuel enrichment process. Refining U_{235} for use in nuclear plants produces U_{238}, or "depleted" uranium. There is nothing depleted about a substance so lethal that it has a half-life as old as this planet: 4.5 billion years. Even before depleted uranium-tipped ordnance was first used in Kosovo in 1999, it contaminated U.S. soils wherever it has been tested and, since then, the soils, water, air, and food chain in Iraq, and at least five other countries where it has been used by the US and its NATO surrogates. According to Samira Abdulghani, in Iraq now, of 100 live births, 15 are of horrifically deformed living beings. Doctors in Iraq have gone on record stating, "Iraq is no longer a place to have children." As early as 1991 DU came home to roost

when returning GIs began complaining of a mysterious set of ailments the VA downplayed as "Gulf Syndrome." Gulf syndrome is radiation sickness by another name The issue of nuclear war is not a remote issue. It is an on-going issue right NOW. Without nuclear plants there can be no nuclear weapons and this is true of "depleted" uranium as well.

The anti-nuclear issue has links to almost every other issue we struggle with today: to the enviro-justice movement, the climate justice movement, and to the fight for economic justice; and because the industry largely exploits people of color and religious minorities both at home and abroad, and adversely affects the health of both atomic workers and people living near nuclear plants, it links up with the labor and anti-racist movements, and to the nonukes movement as well; it connects with gender issues because exposure to radiation is catastrophic to DNA, especially in utero. But MOST OF ALL, because of its secrecy, and fiat decision-making, it links us all together—all of our movements—because it is fundamentally opposed to the democratic process. And that democratic process is where all our struggles MUST converge. That is why, if we can aspire to having any clout, in the face of a government which is becoming more secretive, more autocratic—and more punitive—by the day, we must unite all our movements under this one aegis: the fight to affirm democracy in a country which has lost any intention of ever practicing it.

The keynote address follows. The speaker acknowledges nothing of what my address attempted to point out, not even as he segues into his own talk. It's as though the U.S. 20-year-long war of U238 doesn't exist. Except that what he talks about has everything to do with apologizing to a whale. He describes the twelve men who collaborated, who together are responsible for what has come to be code named The Manhattan Project, the development at Alamogordo of the first atomic bomb. He describes how, before the Trinity test explosion of what was flippantly code named "The Gadget," these men spent days at the blackboard, drawing equations, over and over, trying to get them to "come out right,"—the prerogative of higher mathematicians—in order to reassure themselves that, as they had initially feared, the explosion they were planning would not ignite the atmosphere and blow the world up. ALTHOUGH THERE WAS STILL THE GHOST OF A CHANCE, THEY WENT AHEAD ANYWAY.

That willingness to destroy all life for some imagined "greater good" is the reason I feel obliged to apologize to a whale. It is a phenomenon that has no name. To call it anything, anything at all, reduces the scale of its enormity. No other species in all of the history of life on Earth has ever arrogated to itself such a world-suicidal course. Information is emerging now, even in the mainstream media, that conditions at the site of the 2011 explosions and meltdowns at Fukushima-Daiichi may indeed be the planetary equivalent of atmospheric ignition. The slightest glitch could ignite an unquenchable radiological fire, releasing so much radiation that no work could continue at the site. It would irradiate the Northern Hemisphere, eventually extending to the Southern Hemisphere, contaminating the air, the water, and the soils, and impacting all life on Earth. Whereas atmospheric ignition would have engulfed all living things on the planet in an instantaneous catastrophic extinction, the slightest slipup at Fukushima Daiichi could condemn all living things to slow and agonizing death.

Who were these twelve men, these twelve apostles of apocalypse? What frightened them so that they were willing to blow up worlds? What had they seen? All were men. All were Jewish Europeans. Historically better educated because the tenets of Judaism require literacy, Jews tended to leave the land for towns even before Medieval laws made owning and cultivating land impossible. All twelve shared the same technical formation: physics and mathematics. Coming from a privileged class, they could afford to escape, as millions did not, the great abyss that opened up with the birth of Nazism, and of which they were among its many victims. Most had colleagues left behind in Germany, who were working—despite Hitler's initial resistance to the idea—on developing The Bomb.

On our long drive back from Livermore, we watch a noisy chatter of Canada geese heading across the highway, some 20 individuals, flapping eastward, in V formation, the leader drafting for the others. My eyes follow them until they dip below the skyline. In bed once again, between bouts of spasmodic coughing, I return to this moment. I imagine myself one of the geese. I enter the goose body and for a brief moment I am aloft with my fellows, my wings cutting through dense fog, breasting the chill dawn air. But entering the whale world, entering water, when my own elements are earth where I place my feet, and air which I breathe, inhabiting the deep where I have always feared drowning, is much more difficult—unless I turn the world upside down, imagine for a moment that the air that lofts the geese is water and that my whale flies in air, and that I am flying next to her, looking straight into her great accusing eye.

The twelve men at Alamagordo had recognized in the Germany of their day a national state—much like our present-day United States—which brooked no whistleblowers. Which imprisoned its insurgents and tortured and executed them. It had populations it needed to persecute and to exterminate: gypsies, Catholics, homosexuals—and Jews.

Sophie Scholl was one of those who did not choose to escape. She formed part of the White Rose, a student group which chose to resist Nazism by pamphleteering at the university, in railroad stations and other public venues. Her words attest to her unwavering commitment:

> The real damage is done by those millions who want to "survive." The honest men who just want to be left in peace. Those who don't want their little lives disturbed by anything bigger than themselves. Those with no sides and no causes. Those who won't take measure of their own strength, for fear of antagonizing their own weakness. Those who don't like to make waves—or enemies. Those for whom freedom, honor, truth, and principles are only literature.
>
> Those who live small mate small, die small. It's the reductionist approach to life: if you keep it small, you'll keep it under control. If you don't make any noise, the bogeyman won't find you. But it's all an illusion, because they die too,

those people who roll up their spirits into tiny little balls so as to be safe. Safe?! From what? Life is always on the edge of death; narrow streets lead to the same place as wide avenues, and a little candle burns itself out just like a flaming torch does. I choose my own way to burn.

A small flame snuffed out by her Nazi executioners, a much smaller flame than Trinity.

But it was a woman's flame.

8. Asking the Question

It's always good to start out with a question. Following publication of *Devil's Tango: How I Learned the Fukushima Step by Step* on the first year anniversary of the disaster that has come to be recognized as the most catastrophic industrial accident ever to affect the planet, I toured ten states speaking to thousands of people about Fukushima as it relates to the nuclear industry.

Two years later, and despite the Great Distraction churned up by the mainstream media, the threat of Fukushima has finally surfaced. I feel less called upon to sound the alarm, but out of respect for the deep and very earnest concern of my interlocutors, I want to return to the question they repeatedly voiced: *How can it be that despite sharing the same planet with other living beings, the people who control, and maintain the nuclear industry, are unwilling or unable to acknowledge the catastrophic consequences to the planet of nuclear technology? How can that be?*

I began to ponder the question in light of other intelligences, that is, the intelligences of other-than-human beings who share the planet with *homo sapiens,* the most parasitic animal on earth. I looked there, because unlike humans, animals do not destroy or foul their own nests. I began to think about speech and the use of language as a possible factor because speech (according to humans, but not to other animals) is supposed to be what distinguishes humans from all other animals. What did primates lose when they acquired the power of speech and the use of language? Somehow I intuited that somewhere, wrapped up in the issue of language, we might find an answer.

9. Trade-Offs

To every action there is always an equal and opposite reaction: or the forces of two bodies on each other are always equal and are directed in opposite directions.

—Newton's Third Law of Motion

The long history of human experience seems to bear out Newton's idea of trade-offs.

William Dalrymple's book, *Nine Lives,* chronicles the life of an Indian bard, a storyteller in the ancient sense. Although for nine months of the year he works as a well digger, for three months he travels from village to village singing—by heart— the 5-day-long, 8-hours-a-night epic tale celebrating the god of his own village. He himself is illiterate. Others have tried to learn the epic, but if by chance they acquire literacy, they lose the ability to recite the 40-hour-long epic by heart. It is probably safe to say that every human development perceived as a "gain," must be weighed against a corresponding loss, and that such changes from the very earliest, bipedalism, evolution of the hand and the opposable thumb, to the development of human speech, and the use of language, must have rewired the primate brain.

A step by step exposition of this idea figures in Leonard Shlain's *The Alphabet vs. the Goddess: The Conflict of Word and Image.* His thesis is that wherever in the course of humankind's development literacy appears, the dominant paradigm of the image gives way to the linear organization of the text, and that that point in history coincides with oppression of women.

A comparison of the book's argument laid out in the linear progression of the text itself, can be contrasted with Shlain's video lecture. Many of the book's supporting images, abundantly present in the video, were eliminated by Shlain's publisher in the interests of brevity, but YouTube makes available his abundantly illustrated lecture, providing a valuable example of the differing effect word vs. image produces in the reader/viewer mind.

With certain exceptions, a sentence is strictly linear. For its arrangement of words to be precisely understood, each word temporarily blocks out all other words. It's the same principle as that of an IBM punch card. Each word's meaning is illuminated one at a time. While it is illuminated, all other words are blocked by darkness. For its meaning to emerge, the sentence strings its words along like a necklace strings beads. But the entirety of the *image*—the Gestalt—is global and produces an entire associative field.

In Shlain's lecture, we look, for example, at the image he shares with the viewer in the context of discussing the shift in human affairs to worship of a patriarchal god—here the image by William Blake depicting an ancient, bearded demiurge crouched on threatening clouds circumscribing the world with a compass. We can associate that image with the severity of mosaic law; and if we know Blake, we recognize in it reference to the Newton Blake so hated for his obsession with linear reasoning as the basis of all human knowledge and understanding. That same filter is still embraced by most "educated" people in the western world today, men and women alike, as reflected in such areas as jurisprudence, and in the epistemological constraints of European languages, including English.

Whereas the linear progression of the book's argument stimulates that part of a reader's brain that best processes sequential information, the associative field of the image evokes a whole complex of feelings and ideas. Shlain claims that the very process by which alphabetic literacy is acquired *rewires* the brain favoring the left brain over the right, favoring word, at the expense of image.

In terms of his central thesis, namely that wherever in history literacy appears, that period is oppressive to women, Shlain appears to me to move into somewhat arbitrary grounds.

> I am going to take a leap here. Everyone would agree that both men and women have a feminine side and a masculine side. I am going to give them anatomical mailing addresses: The right hemisphere is the location of most of the feminine instinct we have and the left hemisphere is the seat of the masculine. But there is considerable overlap.

He lends further support to his speculation with a gendered comparison of the rods and cones in the human eye. Rods predominate in the female eye, supporting strong peripheral vision, presumably allowing women to see the big picture—the Gestalt. Cones (which occupy only one percent of the retina), predominate in the male eye, prompting men to zero in on detail. These features, he argues, correspond to the kind of thinking that goes on in the cerebral hemispheres. "We have a feminine way of seeing the world, and a masculine way of seeing the world. Women have more rods, men more cones." These are some of the stepping stones Shlain uses to substantiate his thesis.

However broad Shlain's quantum leap, and however much contemporary research reveals that hemispheric specialization is far more complicated, there is some historic substantiation for his idea. By 800 B.C.—less than 600 years following some of the first evidence of writing—patriarchy had become firmly entrenched in Greece.

The broad implication I take from Shlain's ideas, namely that with every significant breakthrough in the long evolution of human history there may have been an equally significant trade-off, led me to wonder what in the history of human development, beyond bipedalism, may have been the other points of trade-off. Might the acquisition of language be another?

I began to look for it in the behavior and language of animals; I searched for those meeting places in time and space where—very rarely nowadays—animals and humans interact. And I looked at some of the cultures that belong to those we like to refer to as "primitives," that is, people the West considers less "civilized" than ourselves, for what we might have lost.

10. Visit to the Professor

I know very little about Ignacio Chapela except that over some many years his espoused scientific views became so un-orthodox, his very presence had become a challenge to other members of his academic department, ultimately forcing him to sue to retain his job. Speak Now! arranged for him to give a talk at Oakland's Neibyl-Proctor Library. Chapela's project involves re-examining the roots of genetics assumptions: can what one generation learns be inherited by future generations? As his talk progressed I found myself grinning: here was every sign of an original mind at work. He framed his talk by pointing out that there was Science (with a big S) and science. Big Science elaborated its findings on the shoulders of previously accepted assumptions. Little science dared to pause. It dared to question all the assumptions that others might have previously taken for granted, because the true spirit of science is not the publication of scientific papers in prestigious journals, nor is it a quest for careerist advancement. Little science occupies itself with questioning, with turning paving stones over to discover what might lie underneath. The more I listened, the more it occurred to me: Ignacio Chapela might very well be able to suggest how to go about apologizing to a whale.

Dr. Chapela's office window is cut deep into a mansard roof, allowing for a small terrace on which he plants corn, testament to his Mexican heritage, and other cultivars. We shake hands. "It's ten o'clock. There won't be interruptions. It's dead week. We can talk." He invites me to find the most comfortable chair and make myself at home. I outline what I think is my project: where did humankind go wrong? What did primates lose with the acquisition of speech and the use of language? Is that the tipping point? Is that the question I need to ask?

"Well," he says, "if your inquiry is what I think it is, your project is too vague. The tipping point is that place in human prehistory where mankind first discovers agriculture, because that is where Capitalism begins."

I find myself examining the pros and cons of Chapela's reaction. Although he does not assume he fully understands where I am going ("If your inquiry is what I think it is...") and—for the moment at least—neither do I, I do know I am hearing the scientist speaking, hearing someone who requires substantiation, results capable of replication. Does he mean to suggest that the problem first originates with an agrarian population which as it expands requires yet more arable land at the expense of those who *resultingly* are forced to make do with less—or none at all?

But any further discussion with Chapela is interrupted by a knock at the door. One student, two students, soon the room is crammed to bursting. Some 15 chairs are occupied. They've forgone their adolescent sleep—and very shortly after 10 a.m.!—to come visit their professor. One woman is there because later in the morning she is scheduled to speak as part of a seminar requirement. Another woman is there—like me—to bring her project to greater clarity.

Chapela makes room for everyone. He creates an ambiance where everyone feels invited to participate in what becomes an animated discussion, a true *tertulia* in the Latin tradition, a kind of social gathering—in this case with scientific overtones. Here is a master teacher at work, and so adroitly that there is nothing overt or controlling about what happens in that very tiny room. He is the rare academician who is open, fun, and humble enough to be able to meet his students where they are, and to include everyone, myself as well, so much so that the very young ones feel invited to sweep me into their discussion.

It doesn't matter to me that our conversation may have seemed brief. I don't feel in the least deterred or discouraged by his reaction. I have found what I was looking for, namely, that my inquiry will probably be seen from completely different perspectives by almost anyone moved to think about it—and I suspect that many will. And because it has no discernible boundaries, at best, it will have to remain hypothetical. It is not possible to go so far back in time without being open to speculation—and speculation is precisely what it is that draws me.

II.

WORDS BEFORE TALK

11. Learning to Parrot, or How Language Came to Be

Once upon a time, a very long time ago, the Lion, who imagined himself to be King of the Beasts, called a congress of all the animals. The animals laughed behind his back because they knew the Lion was a layabout whose wives did all the hunting. But no matter how much of a poseur he was, the animals knew they always had a good time whenever they got together. So they all showed up at the appointed place and time. The fish came out of the water and the penguins and the whales and the platypus, the pangolin, the shrews, the bears, the birds and buzzards, and all the snakes and turtles. Even the crocodile. The elephants snickered up their trunks because they knew what a fake the Lion was, but they came anyway just for kicks.

When the animals were all assembled, the Lion cleared his throat because he thought it gave him extra majesty. Then he spoke. All of the animals listened politely except for a few birds twittering in the trees.

"We must do something about the Two Legs with their flattened faces. Just when we think we have a nice feast prepared, the Two Legs come along and scare every one of us lions away. Then they crack the bones we haven't got to yet and suck the marrow out! If we don't do something soon they'll steal your dinner too."

The fish thought of their worms, the penguins thought of their fish, the seals thought of their penguins, and the whales thought of their seals.

"And why is that do you suppose?" snapped the Lion's wife.

"Why is that, do you suppose!!! Why is that, do you suppose!!!" The animals repeated her question until it reached the outlying circles of small animals and birds.

The Parrot piped up, "That's easy," he said. "The Two Legs helps himself to what's not his because he can tell everything we say."

The animals listened, amazed at how much surveillance capability the Two Legs really had. A frightened cry went up. "What shall we do?"

"Oh," said the Parrot from his high perch, "that's easy. Leave it to me."

So all of the animals pressed forward to hear what the Parrot had to say. The Parrot struck a pose. "For every cave that caves in, another cave opens. For every tree that falls, another springs up. But it's not the same cave, and it's not the same tree."

Puzzled, the animals looked at one another.

"There's really nothing to it," said the Parrot. "Give the Two Legs a language of his own. He'll be so thrilled with his new toy, he won't remember to see what the sky is telling him. He'll forget to listen when the wind blows. He'll forget to smell what the air tells him. Once he puts a Name to each of our voices, he'll forget everything we say. He won't even hear canaries in the coal mine."

"What's in a Name?" sniffed the Lion.

Piqued, the Parrot turned to the Turtle whose voice was the loudest of the animals. "Speak!" commanded the Parrot.

No sooner had he said it, the Turtle lost her voice. And hard as she tried, all she managed was a hiss.

The animals understood. With a Name, they could see how dumb the Turtle had become. So they sent the Parrot on his way to teach the Two Legs how to put a Name to everything they said, and soon Two Legs learned words like Moo, and Cackle, and Trumpet, and Roar. And pretty soon he forgot what the sky was telling him. When the Earth trembled, he forgot what it said. He forgot to listen when the wind blew. He forgot to smell what the air was telling him.

And he stopped hearing the canaries sing.

12. Mankind Once Spoke With A Single Tongue . . .

of brotherly love, we sweetly sung
but love meant one thing to you, Marat,
and something quite different to me.

—Peter Weiss: *Marat-Sade*

The discovery of fire, and how to use it to cook, may have been at play in the development of human language and of speech. Once strong jaws and teeth were no longer required to tear apart raw meat, canine teeth could recede from dominance. Neck, jaw, and facial muscles could realign themselves. But the use of words, and the development of language could not emerge until the morphology of jaw and neck could support vocal chords, and such musculature could not develop before primates stood upright. The whooping and howling and screaming of beasts could be left behind after a few million years or so, and the ape countenance flattened until at last it could be recognized as the beginnings of a human face.

In all probability, the first group of languages spoken by human primates was one of three click languages known as Khoisan, which is still spoken thousands of years later by the San (see Section 21), whom geneticists have determined were the first to branch off from the original human mitochondrial tree.

Whales and orcas also have their language of clicks and whistles and hums, and each pod has its dialect. Mothers teach the vocabulary to their offspring, who learn how to embellish the sound structures from a basic vocabulary as they mature. Clans of the same species swim separately, and do not share the same language, and occasionally when a community gathers in a superpod, each clan's language remains opaque to every other. Throughout the year, the entire humpback pod sings the identical song, but the song changes from year to year in such a way that gradually, over time, as hums and groans and clicks are transformed, the songs become increasingly dissimilar. Audiographs of humpback songs recorded from 1972 through 1979 off the coast of Maui by Katy Payne (see Section 14: Two Mind Job) clearly document these transitions.

13. The Art of Un-Naming

Show me your face before you were born.
—Buddhist Koan

Although I never attended writing school, because I had published a novel or two, it was assumed that I might have something to say about what goes by the rubric Creative Writing. (Now that I find myself officially in retirement, I can safely say that Creative Writing is a scam. No one can teach another how to write. The only writing school I ever attended is called Reading. Such observations, however, do not preclude the possibility of offering students guidance and encouragement in finding their own voices based on their individual, very unique ways of seeing the world.) The prospect of official employment mesmerized me into eventually applying to a search committee for a teaching job. To back up my pedagogical credentials, I aired my convictions: humans are born knowing everything they need to know. Not unexpectedly, I had to wait till I reached 63 years of age to be offered my first professional opportunity to earn a living wage, an advantage that has become increasingly obsolete for most of my countrymen and women (note the privileging of the masculine).

In the course of my workshops, a student once shared a short story in which she identified one of her characters as a "bum." A conversation about naming ensued. What happens when we name a character? So doing, are we doing the work of the reader? Are we telling the reader because we don't have imagination enough to show him? or her? (Notice the way the language you are reading at this moment privileges the male every time a third-person singular pronoun is used.) And once we do the reader's work, is the story over as such because to be authentic, narrative must remain a negotiation in which writer and reader play their parts—a concept, incidentally, not out of line with democracy itself.

Over many years I have been collecting stories describing animal behavior (obviously from the viewpoint of human observers). Only recently, however, Marina Chapman, a woman in her early fifties now living in England, published her "as-told-to" book, *The Girl With No Name*,* detailing the years she survived as a very young child, living in the jungle somewhere along the border between Colombia and Venezuela. Although she makes no mention of it, the time coincides with the beginning of the conflict (aided and abetted by U.S. and CIA intervention) between the Colombian government and two resistance movements, the Revolutionary Armed Forces of Colombia (the FARC) and the National Liberation Army (the ELN).

Marina Chapman describes being seized at the approximate age of five while playing in her family's allotment garden by kidnappers who probably chloroformed her and carried her off blindfolded in some kind of vehicle. Evidently the kidnapping must have turned sour, and her abductors ditched her in the jungle where, for roughly five years, she would find a home living among a troop of silver capuchin monkeys.

Although she writes to appeal to popular tastes, the story itself seems to me extremely valuable in that it involves a human narrator whose ideas are not yet fully formed. The five-year-old human brain is still a learning organ, able to absorb, open to learning from observation of yet unnamed things and beings. Hers is an account free of the dictates of culture or the strictures of mores, and the more rigidly controlled observations of animal behaviorists, people who observe animals because that is their professional calling, or who as adults, many of them, may suffer from predetermined ideas, or have something to gain, or may simply adhere to a sharper sense of species categorization.

---

*I found this article from *The Guardian* to be rich on background: http://www.theguardian.com/science/2013/apr/13/marina-chapman-monkeys

Chapman describes her initial loneliness and fear as she struggles to find food. Some few days of searching lead her to a location which she discovers is the habitat of a troop of capuchins. At first they remain aloof but tolerant of her presence, but from them she learns what is edible, although she bridles at eating orchids, grasses, and lizards. One day, mistaking a bean pod for tamarind, she becomes violently ill. Although he has never approached her before, the patriarch of the clan seizes her by the hair and begins dragging her to the brink of a steep hill, forcing her to tumble downward into a basin filled with brackish water. He follows and tries to push her head under. Afraid of drowning, she fights back violently. At the height of their struggle, he pulls her face upward, forcing her to look him straight in the eyes. She describes his expression:

> As I looked back at him, I could see something I hadn't before. His expression was completely calm. It wasn't angry, or agitated or hostile.... Perhaps he was trying to tell me something.... I didn't know what it was, but in that instant I trusted him. The look in his eyes and the calmness in his movements made me realize he was trying to help me.

Once the patriarch forces her to drink the brackish water, she is able to vomit until her stomach empties. Afterwards, he edges her to another part of the pool where he makes her drink the fresh water trickling from a waterfall. After a protracted period of recovery she feels strong enough to clamber back up the slope. But most remarkably, the patriarch waits with her for all the time it takes her to recover, scurrying back up the slope only when he sees she is ready to move. This encounter becomes a turning point in her coexistence with the clan, whose members now begin to relate to her physically, trusting her enough to touch her and groom her, and allow her to join in their play and carry the young ones when they climb up on her shoulders.

By the time, roughly five years later, Chapman makes human contact (a much less fortunate turn of events), she has forgotten human language; but by observation she has learned to understand the cries and vocalizations of monkeys, which, now in her fifties, she is still able to replicate. Because she was able to distinguish the troop's cry for danger, she was able to discover that—just for fun—the juveniles delighted in fooling their elders from time to time once they had learned to imitate the cry.

She describes a clan whose behavior was consistently peaceful and cooperative—except on those rare occasions when an alien clan invaded its territory. In those instances the surviving monkeys, whom she had known as peaceful and nurturing of family, came down from the canopy with their teeth bloodied and their bodies gashed with wounds.

14. The Charged Border: Playing With Whales

In the beginning, we are told, God created the heavens and Earth. Although not always one to attend to unfinished business, nonetheless by the third day, God managed to separate the dry land from the waters, and territory (a derivative of *terra* from the Latin, meaning earth or land) was born. As my Polish-Jewish uncle-in-law used to say: "So far, so good." He was a chemist and he ought to know.

But in the fluid world of oceans, does a concept such as territoriality apply? Is there a corresponding imperative in those highly intelligent beings who inhabit the deep? How do mammals such as the pseudo-orcas, whales, and dolphins, relate to the vast spaces they inhabit? Do cetaceans—and fish for that matter—stake out ownership and defend it against all comers? Do species war with other species over fishing grounds? Or do they observe boundary "agreements"?

More than anyone alive, with the possible exception of Jacques Cousteau, Jim Nollman has inhabited the deep, and returned to tell of it. He calls that area where humans and animals meet "the charged border," the title of his 1999 book of the same name. In it, he juxtaposes reports of his encounters with a number of cetacean species, and with people whom he meets and with whom he works, whose pursuits range from the strictly scientific to New Age dolphin-based mysticism. Nollman tests his ideas against this wide spectrum of folks, and in the process, the reader comes to trust him and his voice.

Although he does not claim to be a natural scientist so much as a musician, Nollman began a cultural experiment designed to investigate how music might affect cetaceans whose migration and feeding patterns brought them in close proximity to an island off the coast of Vancouver.

Like any beginner, he learned by doing, initially making the human-dominator mistake of intervening in contacts that had occurred spontaneously at first. He discovered that if through his music, he was to initiate dialogue with these beings, it would be on *their* terms or not at all. But, unlike the scientists he met along the way who were undeviatingly wedded to perceptions colored by their own "expertise," Nollman seems to have had the awareness of the artist, able to cede control, as all musicians learn to do when they become truly ensemble players. Once he discovered the need to pay attention to whale intentionality, he was able to participate in the kind of encounters that take his—and the reader's—breath away.

In a boat riding at anchor, he installed acoustic arrays with underwater speakers. If whale song has offered striking clues to whale behavior, why not reverse the story and make music for whales?

Nollman describes how playing a simple musical phrase outside the whale's own repertoire sometimes produced an unforeseen result. At first he spent two nights trying the same twelve-bar blues riff on his electric guitar. On the third night, a young bull, identified by his neighbor researchers as "A-6," began to join in, improvising over Nollman's chord progression. The whale kept his accompaniment harmonically and rhythmically consistent, and recognized chord changes on the correct downbeats. Nollman describes A-6's phrasing as austere, maybe fifteen notes to the verse. But then, as the second verse started, Nollman initiated a burst of single notes. Within four more bars, A-6 resumed his normal whale patterns of vocalization and vanished. But what's really interesting is that, although the pod remained for the most part indifferent, A-6 kept coming back, accompanied now by his mother, A-2, who, perhaps because they found her the most friendly and outgoing whale of the pod, the local researchers were drawn to name Nickola. Both whales kept returning and jamming with Nollman, but some months later, following Nickola's death, A-6 lost interest and never came back. Perhaps I am reading into it, but I infer in this account a kind of curiosity, possibly cultural eagerness on Nickola's part to encourage contact, and to prompt her son to explore it with her. I see in her behavior the traditional prompting role of the cetacean matriarch.

During three summers, Tibetan lamas came to chant Buddhist prayers directly into the water through the underwater speakers. Although most of the orcas seemed indifferent, two whales repeatedly lagged behind as the rest of the pod swam up the strait. They would grow silent, and come near, apparently listening. But the most dramatic encounters occurred some summers later. Several pods gathered into a superpod, mingling and mating as a single extended family. At the time, Nollman had taken to improvising on Indian ragas. During the next several days, unusual things began to happen: two whales swam up between boat and shore, stirring up the waves, lighting up the cove with bioluminescent plankton. Next afternoon, to the accompaniment of the same raga, all forty-seven whales circled just outside the cove. At one point, not one hundred yards distant from the boat, fourteen of them sky-hopped in unison. But when the unusual agglomeration of the extended family disbanded, Nollman was no longer able to engage any of them with his playing.

The first lesson he learned was one of the respect that comes with learning deep listening, recognition that there is no way to know another's consciousness, and that one must be open to surprises, and willing to cede power and the sense of anthropocentric superiority in all its manifestations. Call this **Lesson One.**

By contrast, a recent Nova special, "How Smart Are Animals?", provides an excellent example of anthropomorphic chauvinism. Condescending in tone, it defines animal "intelligence" as the ability to read (and obey!) human cues. At one point a so-called scientist defines compliant dogs as being "just like soldiers," eager to fulfill the experimenter's every command. Ultimately, it becomes fascinating to perceive the humans behaving as though they were the subjects of their own experiments, acting in predictably unimaginative ways, actually colonizing the minds of animals while imagining that they are demonstrating animal "intelligence." Finally, the best measure of an animal's intelligence, according to Nova, is the degree of slavishness displayed by that animal's behavior.

I am reminded of a time in 1971 when the experimental theater company I directed was rehearsing *The Serpent* by Jean-Claude van Itallie. We knew the famous Becks of the Living Theater were coming to town. We had raised money to help spring them from the Brazilian jail where the generals of the Brazilian dictatorship had imprisoned them, and we packed the theater *en masse*, eager to hear what they had to say of their time working in Brazil.

For people of the theater world, the Becks held an iconic place as initiators of a theater so *avant garde* it shocked Americans to their very roots. But the Becks themselves, Julian and Judith, were New York Jews who were raised in the middle class milieu of New York's West End Avenue where, in their first years, they mounted performances in people's living rooms. But what they did later was certainly not living room theater.

In the 100-seat San Francisco theater they spoke of the redemptive work they had initiated in the *favelas* of Rio de Janeiro. They were quick to determine that the impoverished slum dwellers living there suffered from mother complexes (although perhaps not the same mother complexes afflicting the Jewish middle class of West End Avenue). At the back of the audience, in the standing-room-only section, was a man who was clearly living an alternate reality. Whether he was high on drugs, or living in a parallel world, I don't know to this day, but the more I watched, the more I became convinced he was performing a kind of schizoid sign language, reflecting what I was coming to feel with growing impatience was the Becks' culturally arrogant take on a poor and very marginalized society. As I watched, a curious thing began to happen. Audience and speakers both took on the quality of performance. The evening wore on, the theater became uncomfortably hot and stuffy. At last, the proceedings came to a momentary stop when a woman raised a timid hand to ask: "But what did you learn from *them?*"

Nollman describes two "nations" (cultures really) of orcas (which are popularly referred to as "killer whales" by folks who drink the Marineland/TV/Disney KoolAid), feeding off the coast of Vancouver. One "nation" inhabits the waters year round and vocalizes with a variety of sounds; they kill only what they eat. The other nation he refers to as transients, beings who range over wide stretches of ocean. They have a completely different culture. Although these beings are of *exactly the same* genetic species, they have not crossbred in 100,000 years, and their *languages* (consisting of whistles, clicks and hums) *are incomprehensible* one nation to the other. Their habits are very different. They almost never whistle because they rely on stealth to capture their prey. They eat only the tongues. Once satisfied, they maim the bodies, severing the dorsal fins with one four-foot bite, before discarding them.

The world's power arrangements reveal a parallel dissonance: on September 5, 2013, despite a more than 60 percent popular opposition to engaging in yet another war, the administration of the United States, represented by its Secretary of State and availing itself of the same trumped up demagoguery that led to the Afghan and Gulf invasions of 1990, 2001, and 2003, and "regime change" of our former ally, Muhammar Quaddafi in Libya, voted in committee 10 to 7 to engage in a "limited" attack on Syria. The resolution carried a sixty-day authorization limit with a possible 30-day extension. (During the three hours the Secretary of State took to make the case for war Senator John McCain, a member of the committee, played solitaire on his iPod—and lost.) Imagining that once engaged, hostilities could be stopped on the dime of a "90 days later" stipulation indicates the degree to which the U.S. administration has become a delusional body in contrast to the larger body still calling itself humanity. The larger body is well aware it harbors a malignancy, but the malignant cells themselves behave without insight—as cancer cells tend to do.

In general, the seas are mapped by its mammals, not so much for possession, but for feeding and reproduction. They mate in due season; bear their young, migrate year after year from sea to sea along established routes. If they attack, their purpose is to eat. If they fight it is to secure a mate. Juvenile whales have been observed mock fighting to develop their skills for later competition for a mate. When the fighting becomes too rough, they break off, reassemble in a daisy configuration, and calm down with their heads at the center of their circle facing one another.

At anchor off Vancouver, Nollman is thrown in with scientists whose expertise involves counting the numbers in various pods, identifying each individual by number, and darting them—surely an uncomfortable if not painful invasion of cetacean privacy. Their worldviews collide in expected ways, yet they persist in dialogue—they have little choice, cooped up as they are for long stretches in the small boat they use as their experimental headquarters.

One university-affiliated scientist summers close by, kayaking daily in the waters to observe marine life. He never misses identifying the cetaceans he watches day after day as "dumb animals." And yet, once a year for the past three years, his sleep is interrupted by the mortar-loud sound of whales blowing very near to shore. He puts on his gear, takes a flashlight to discover a huge king salmon, thrashing so high that it looks to him as though the orcas were able to chip it like a golf ball way up onto the gravel beach directly fronting his tent. This ritual happens only at night. Only one salmon, one salmon a year. The first year it happens, the scientist dismisses it as an accident, the second year, it's still an accident. By the third year he has become subdued. "Why me?" he fairly whispers, "when I'm the guy that harasses them all day long."

Nollman also spends considerable time in the company of eco-tourists bent on making contact with dolphins and who hope to swim with them in the Sea of Cortez under the direction of their tour leader, an artist named Carolyn, because with few exceptions, they are convinced of the "spiritual dimensions" of human-with-dolphin "vibrational" communication. Throughout their time together, Nollman identifies what he refers to as Carolyn's guardedness—some might call it defensiveness—in response to his challenges. His skepticism lends weight to his own observations. Nevertheless, he witnesses a tourist lazing belly up on deck, hat covering his eyes, sitting up suddenly to declare, "Three dolphins told me they'll be arriving from the south in ten minutes." Nollman reports that fifteen minutes later, three dolphins appeared from out of the south. He eventually sheds his skepticism enough to ask Carolyn what dolphins tell her. Carolyn's reply: "That we humans need to see ourselves as spiritual entities who inhabit physical bodies for just a short time. My dolphin friend doesn't care if she dies tomorrow.... Except we don't accept it, and she does."

According to one of Gödel's theorems, a smaller processor can't map the capacities of a larger processor. Applied to cetaceans in particular, the human brain is too puny to begin to conceive of whale brain complexity. For example, sperm whales are unique among the toothed whales for clicking back and forth to one another. This behavior has prompted observers to speculate that they use echolocation to talk to one another, possibly using its three-dimensionality to share kinetic, holographic story memes in a language impossible for the human brain to begin imagining.

To attract females, humpback whales, unique among baleen whales, sing complex songs consisting of eighteen-minute-long melodies, which seem to undergo gradual modification from year to year. Some twenty years after his first observations, Roger Payne and his associate Linda Guinee found that the verses of these songs actually ended in rhymes, perhaps for the same reason that human epic poems use rhymes to help their bards recite them from memory. This ability may indicate that whales actually understand the building blocks of language. When SETI researcher and astronomer Laurance Doyle, along with his colleagues at UC Davis and the Alaska Whale Foundation, applied to whale song the mathematics of information theory they discovered that humpback vocalizations demonstrate rule structure complexity, indicating that they, along with humans, are subject to rules of syntax. Often a humpback virtuoso may attract an audience, usually of females, perhaps implying what Nollman calls "a species-specific sense of aesthetics." Roger Payne actually speculates that such songs may be humpback epic poems describing the lineage of the singer, *and* in rhymed verse!

According to Nollman, in the Marine Mammal Laboratory at Hawaii's Kewalo Basin, bottlenose dolphins have mastered 60 English words and basic grammatical rules that allow them to put together nouns, verbs and direct and indirect objects to understand hundreds of simple sentences. One of the commands they understand is the word "creative." If they hear "tandem creative," they come together in an apparent formation and perform a movement in tandem. Nollman can only describe it in human words: "[they] presumably agree on an action. The question is how do they come to synchronize it? Do they use clicks and whistles to agree together, do they use vibrational communication of a dolphin sort? Or do they use some other modality entirely?"

I know something about initiating such "modalities" from my twelve years as an experimental theater director, developing works in a collective process of ensemble creation. When my company had become so finely tuned through trust and ensemble exercises, (that is when it had created its own non-verbal language) it was entirely capable—and here I am talking of a company of anywhere from 15 to 19 actors—to go from synchronizing their breathing into an "action" characterized by a rhythmic arc that might last as long as fifteen and sometimes even twenty minutes.

Cooperative fishing among humpbacks might offer another example—this one in the wild—of such unrehearsed "modalities." Once a humpback senses a school of herring, it gives a signal to other members of its pod. As many as twenty individuals might answer the call by swimming closely together. The team dives directly underneath the herring and swims in circles, releasing a curtain of bubbles that rise in the water column, creating a kind of bubble net. The turbulence catches the herring as effectively as if the humpbacks had used a purse seine. Once the herring are corralled, the humpbacks rise inside their net and, just before breaking the surface, they open their great mouths to suck in tons of herring.

Nollman cites stories of aboriginal people whose "dreaming," i.e., totem, is the bottlenose dolphin and who, living by the sea, have had the leisure of thousands of years of observing them and passing on their discoveries to later generations until their body of knowledge of dolphin behavior is every bit as informed as that of any marine biologist, but with the objective not so much of gathering data but rather out of concern for tribal food security and personal power. Eventually, they have been able to negotiate a collaborative process—call it channeling—or vibrational communication if you will—of cooperative fishing with the dolphins. Nollman cites two accounts, both involving tribal shamans:

> When I was a small boy, I used to go fishing with my uncle who had studied the dolphins for many years. When he called to them usually three dolphins would spread out at the sides of the boat and another one at the back. They would make a field of sounds and drive a whole mob of fish up onto the shore. He knew so many sounds and the exact way to do it; and sometimes he would take up some salt water in the palm of his hand, and clap his hands together in a certain way to tell the dolphins what kind of fish he was hunting for that day.

And this:

> One day we were walking along the Ggodiggah near Walpardi. My Daddy sang the sacred song even though there was only one dolphin there. I went away, I never believed my Daddy. I didn't take any notice of him singing. I had my own spear and so I went up on the hill and there were all the boys there. And this one boy, he comes over and says, "Hey! You look over there. All them dolphins are everywhere!" Where they come from I don't know. And at that time we

were all hungry because we had no fish. And all of a sudden I couldn't believe my eyes. All the fish, black everywhere in the waves! And my Daddy was singing the song for the dolphins. He walks along the beach and he whistles like this (makes a slow vibrating whistle)....And after that my Daddy does this (slow clapping). And the dolphin come right up and my Daddy threw [one] fish to the dolphin.

Observes Nollman, "Traditional cultures that rely on channeling for their perception of the sacred have always been discounted as less enlightened than our own." He quotes anthropologist Paul Reisman:

> Our social sciences treat the culture and knowledge of other peoples as forms and structures necessary for human life that those people have developed and imposed upon a reality which we know—or at least our scientists know—*better* than they do. We can therefore study those forms in relation to reality and measure how well or ill they are adapted to it. In their studies of the cultures of other people, even those anthropologists who sincerely love the people they study almost never think that they are learning something about the way the world really is. Rather they conceive of themselves as finding out what *other* people's conceptions of the world are [itals. added].

Nollman continues: "The practices of traditional culture confirm the virtues of interdependence. Native people observed other species closely, seeking practical insight to help meet their own life challenges. Unhampered by the hierarchical organization that positions one species above or below another, they had great freedom to learn from every species. By contrast, our anthropocentric society has not yet learned that *the prevailing 'separate and not equal' worldview is killing the planet and us along with it*" [itals. added].

Have whales learned to respond to messages they are somehow able to pick up from humans? As a young boy, future naturalist Farley Mowat had never seen a whale. Out sailing with his dad off Nova Scotia, they were about to head for home when a dense fog obliterated all navigational signs. Navigating blind, they risked running aground on coastal reefs. They dropped anchor. Young Mowat took the midnight watch. On the verge of falling asleep, he was startled awake by an ungodly sound reverberating through the air, the boat, and his very being. He sensed such a sound could only be coming from a whale. Awakened from a deep sleep, his father joined him aft. Again the whale "spoke" but at a farther distance indicating it was headed south-southwest. Father and son got the idea that it might very well be leading them toward home. Able to cruise at barely 2 to 3 knots against the wind, they realized the whale seemed to be slowing its normal speed to allow them to follow. They reached the channel buoy at daylight, where once again the whale "spoke" its "ungodly" farewell before swimming out to sea.

Is it idle to speculate whether there may be some unknown wavelength to explain such an uncanny event, and if such communication may possibly be a two way street? The film "Blackfish" features First Nations people of the Northwest who have lived close to orcas for generations. They consider what they call the black fish a being of infinite power and wisdom. One of the marine biologists appearing in the film states that the orcas' sense of identity is the pod itself. Their collaborative social behavior shows the organization one expects to find in a colony such as the Portuguese man-of-war where three individuals bound together act in concert, behaving as one system. To illustrate this point, the film shows a whale-hunting expedition off the coast of Washington State (from which such hunts were eventually banned for their cruelty) where young orca calves are hunted by boat and plane for capture and sale to marine amusement parks throughout the world. Aware that it is being hunted, the pod separates. The males act as decoys, luring the ship away from the females and their young to allow them to escape. But the relentless search by plane defeats the pod's purpose. At the conclusion of the episode, three of the whales are dead, and wailing females are surrounded by all the pod's individuals, who refuse to abandon the captured young.

Although in the wild, the young remain close to their mothers throughout their lives, marine amusement park entrepreneurs breed orcas to be sold for profit. When they are old enough, the young calves are wrenched away from their mothers. The wails of anguish and desolation of the bereft mothers are agonizing to hear, so much so that viewing this episode recently made me realize in a way that previously had escaped me the full horror of present-day mass deportations (two million people during the present administration) and some estimated two million* similar incidents in the antebellum south where slave families were torn apart, sometimes separating children from their mothers and transferring their ownership to others for a profit.*

Are whales trying to send us a message? In April, 2004, when she heard on the 6:00 o'clock news that three men had been killed in Iraq, Cindy Sheehan fell to the ground screaming. She knew with certainty one of those men was her son. His death was to devastate her life; she nearly died of hemorrhage and her marriage fell apart. Although she lives in Sacramento, California, Cindy Sheehan first came to public attention when in the name of her son, Casey, she established a peace camp in close proximity to Bush's dude ranch in Crawford, Texas, demanding to know what was "the just cause for which my son had to die?"

In the same month that she learned of Casey's death, a whale was reported to be swimming up the Sacramento River accompanied by her calf. While crowds lined the riverbanks, hoping for a glimpse, no one thought to wonder if perhaps she wasn't "lost" at all, but that somehow she may have been bringing her calf upriver with her, in response to Cindy's grief.

Frank Robson is one of the very first non-scientists to explore cetacean communication. He worked for some years as a trainer in a New Zealand oceanarium. His description comes

---

Help Me to Find My People by Heather Williams estimates that a coincidental two million enslaved people were wrenched from their families to be sold and transported—some from the auction block in Washington D.C., at the present site of the U.S. Department of Justice.

closest to identifying the substance of interspecies communication. During the month Nollman spent with him, he revealed how when he wished to get his dolphins to perform a trick, "he visualized the picture of them doing the trick in his mind." Robson described it thus:

> [It's] a vibration that reflects. It's not unlike walking in the dark and stopping at an obstruction without actually seeing it. With animals it's a two-mind job. Until the mind that you are trying to reach is receptive to what you've got to transmit, it's hopeless."

15. Two-Mind Job

Although Katy Payne came to Portland to participate in a biologists' conference, she happened to be in the Portland Zoo because three baby elephants had been born, and she wanted to see them. As she stood in the elephant house contemplating one of its huge inhabitants, she became aware of a strange sensation, a feeling she likened to experiencing the rumble of an organ's lowest notes, something she had felt as a 13-year-old attending church. Later it occurred to her that the sound might have been coming from the elephant standing before her, and that in some way, it had been trying to communicate with her.

She came to wonder if whales could make infrasonic sounds not readily distinguishable to human ears, why couldn't elephants do the same? As she herself says, "I never really grew up. Children are aware of all kinds of things that they close themselves to when they grow up. In that week, when I was sitting in the zoo, I was just a child again, and all possibilities were open to me...." On the night of her discovery she had a dream:

> I dreamed that I was surrounded by elephants. Now, at that time, I had only seen Asian elephants in a zoo.... I was surrounded by African elephants on a flat piece of savanna. And

they were reaching out to me with their trunks, sniffing me the way elephants do. And then the matriarch of the group spoke.... I heard the words...in English, because that's what I understand. And she said, "We did not reveal this to you so that you would tell other people." So I woke knowing that the elephants had revealed it to me, not that I had discovered something.

As a student, Katy Payne developed an interest in biology; her love of music dates from even earlier in her life. But no matter how abstract her studies, on graduation from college she realized she would have to make her way in the world. Her deep knowledge of whale song came about because throughout their 32 years of whale research, she was married to Roger Payne, with whom she released a record, "Songs of the Humpback Whale." Much like Rachel Carson's work, this recording made Americans more aware of the natural world—and whales in particular— where before they had not paid very much attention. (Examples of these sounds can be heard at http://www.onbeing.org/program/ whale-songs-and-elephant-loves/feature/communication-wild-recordings-katy-paynes-research.) Now she identifies herself as a self-trained acoustic biologist. More than recording and analyzing animal sounds, more than travelling vast distances to hear and analyze them, at the very root of her work, Katy Payne is a listener. It helps to know that she is a practicing Quaker.

I must have been six or seven years of age when I experienced attending a Quaker meeting. My parents, convinced that keeping a child cooped up in New York City during its unbearably hot summers was tantamount to child abuse, farmed me out to a Quaker woman who kept a "baby farm" in Tuckerton, New Jersey, at that time a sleepy little village. One Sunday she took me along when she went to "meeting." But "meeting" was nothing like what I knew from the times earlier in life when my father had taken me to Catholic Church to sit in the stiflingly hot balcony while Mass was in progress. At this meeting, there was no balcony. Everyone sat in rows facing everyone else. It was a church so old it smelled of mouse droppings, with beautiful high

Georgian windows, and not much else. People sat silently. If "the spirit moved them," they stood and spoke. I found the silence, the heat, the buzz of flies uncomfortable. I spoke. I stood up to affirm that God was everywhere. I knew this to be certain because every time I passed my church, even if the doors were closed, I could see the sanctuary light burning through the transom. No one reproved me until much later when we were well out of earshot, but I remember that after "meeting," the two elders, the man and wife who presided, shook my hand as they shook the hands of all who had lined up. I took this for approval. I had never seen anyone quite like these elders or quite so old. The man's clothes made him look like Abraham Lincoln, and, except for the lady's poke bonnet, they could have posed for "American Gothic." But most of all I remember the silences, where everyone listened for "the spirit to move them."

Above all else, Payne* recognizes that listening forms an integral part of elephant behavior:

> [Elephants] do something…that I wish we [did] more of the time.., something you find in Quaker [and Buddhist] meetings…as well. The whole herd, and it may be 50 animals, will suddenly be still, completely still. And it's not just a stillness of voice; it's a stillness of body. So you'll be watching the moving herd, they'll be all over the place, they'll be facing all directions, doing different things. Suddenly everything freezes as if a movie was turned into a still photograph, and the freeze may last a whole minute, which is a long time. They're listening. When they freeze, they tighten and lift and spread their ears. This tells us…that they're concerned with what's going on over the horizon.

She describes elephants as emotional and passionate:

> If there's an animal that is, on the whole, more emotional than human beings, it's elephants. They have fits of delight

---

*"On Being," Kirsta Tippett interviews Katy Payne, http://www.onbeing. org/program/whale-songs-and-elephant-loves/particulars/346.

and fits of frustration, and, when a group of elephants that has been separated even for a few hours comes together [they act as as if] they'd been apart for years. But actually, it [might be] only since 10 o'clock in the morning. They rush together, twirl their trunks together, roar, urinate, defecate, flap their ears, and the whole thing says that each individual is overcome with excitement.

And they are capable of deep sorrow and compassion:

> We witnessed the death of a young calf. This baby had come in with her mother repeatedly. She was very thin and weak, and on that day we knew she was going to die. She lay down and within a couple of hours…she had died. [For two days…] more than 100 elephants, unrelated to the calf, walked past the place where the little corpse lay on the ground…. Some of them took a detour around [her]. About a quarter of them tried to lift the body up with their tusks and their trunks…. One adolescent male attempted to lift up this little corpse fifty-seven times, and walked away from it and came back five different times. [And] these were not related animals….

But Katy Payne has company. The March 11, 2014 *Scientific American* carried an article by Matt Kaplan reporting on the work of biologists Karen McComb, Graeme Shannon, and Fritz Vollrath, showing that elephants are not just good listeners, but they are discriminating about what they hear, recognizing language difference, i.e. ethnicity, human gender *and* age in terms of evaluating potential danger to themselves and identifying possible attackers. They huddle together especially tightly when they hear Maasai, "even though spearings by Maasai have declined in recent years," because the young "follow the lead of their matriarchs who remember such spearings from long ago." They are less likely to huddle or flee from people speaking Kamba, or from women, or from boys, although herds led by matriarchs younger than 42 retreat from boys about 40 percent of the time.

16. Saving Elephants and Other Non-Human Persons

Two years following the BP Deep Water Horizon disaster in the Gulf of Mexico, the University of California at Berkeley signed an agreement with BP to establish an Energy Biosciences Institute to fund (as university PR proclaimed) research in alternative energies. Described by Chris Hedges in *Empire of Illusion*, the deal with BP for $500 million allows BP "access to the university's researchers and technological capacity, built by decades of public investment.... [Under this agreement] BP can shut down another research center and move into a publicly subsidized one. BP will receive intellectual property rights, which it can use for profit, on scientific breakthroughs expected to come out of the joint project."

With many others, I opposed the arrangement. I do not feel corporations have a place in any institution of learning. Despite the warning of Eisenhower's parting words, "Beware of the military-industrial-*academic* complex," [itals. added for accuracy] the history of corporate—and government—links to American universities have brought us napalm (Harvard), agent orange (University of Chicago) and nuclear weapons (University of California). Two of the 24 labs planned for the BP-sponsored Energy Biosciences Institute, presumably devoted to alternative energies, will investigate how to "enhance the recovery of petroleum from underground reserves" and how to "use microbes to process coal into fuel."

Nor am I blind to the pressures of rising tuition that most students who want to attend this once-public university have to accept, although many of them will have difficulty finding jobs in this economy, and upon graduation will become indentured servants for life, some with as much as $150,000, even $200,000, owing on their student loans.

Since 2007, at least seven major construction sites have been active on campus at any one time, some of them fought bitterly by residents of the city of Berkeley whose environmental awareness did not allow them to forget the 2010 industrial catastrophe described by BP as a "spill" in the Gulf of Mexico. Ever since, I have found it increasingly difficult to overcome my reluctance to avail myself of the many resources this campus has to offer.

Recently I overcame my reluctance. On my way to the graduate library, I entered the campus at noontime. Sproul Plaza was lined as usual with a row of tables to either side of the walkway where sororities, fraternities, and various campus groups set up their recruiting tables. This is the campus that saw huge demonstrations in 1964 during the Free Speech movement, when the issue was obtaining the right to share political messages on campus, and to mount demonstrations to end the Vietnam War. Now, at a time when the U.S. government is threatening another illegal war, this one in the eastern Mediterranean, at a time when political fault lines in the Middle East have built up the kind of pressure which has the very real potential of igniting World War III, or IV, depending on who's counting, this campus displays the level of critical thinking and political expression one might have expected to see in the somnolescent 50s.

As I walk the table gauntlet, one student hands me a palm-sized flyer:

MARCH FOR ELEPHANTS:
ELEPHANTS ARE IN CRISIS!
35,000 KILLED LAST YEAR BY POACHERS
HUGE DEMAND FROM CHINA FOR IVORY TUSKS
EXTINCTION LESS THAN 10 YEARS AWAY

I turn the flyer over. The statistics it cites stagger the mind: Elephant herds in Africa have been depleted from 1.3 million in 1979 to about 300,000 today. At the kill rate of 100 elephants per day (up 30 percent from last year), extinction is projected by 2020. Most poachers work in organized criminal gangs killing elephants—and here's the claim—"to fund terrorist organizations, illegal drug trade and human trafficking." Whenever I see the combination of "terrorism," drugs, and human trafficking, I have learned from previous examples, notably those of Colombia,

Afghanistan, and Mexico, to suspect that U.S. covert interference may very well be involved.

I am reminded that war is the weapon of industrialized nations; terror is the weapon of otherwise defenseless—and often very poor—people. Although there is no mention anywhere of AFRICOM, the U.S. projection of its imperial power over Africa, I wonder at the coincidence. It's not easy to use the March for Elephants website. Only by studying the blog site do I learn that this apparently very well-funded effort is an offshoot of the David Sheldrike Wildlife Trust. As part of its fundraising campaign, the website cites the remarkable story surrounding Lawrence Anthony's death.

17. The Elephant Whisperer

Co-author with his brother-in-law of the eponymously titled book, Lawrence Anthony was born and died in South Africa only fairly recently. Grandson of a Scots miner, and son of an insurance entrepreneur, he grew up in the veldt in Zambia, Malawi, before finally settling in Zululand, and although fluent in English, Afrikaans, and in Zulu, he never finished high school. Despite his deeply felt connection to the landscape and to all natural life, he followed his father into the insurance business before becoming a highly successful real estate developer. At the pinnacle of his commercial career, together with his wife, he decided to chuck it all when the unusual opportunity to buy a game reserve came his way. The story goes that, following his death 800 miles away in Johannesburg, the elephants back home in Thula Thula, his game reserve, walked a whole day in single file from deep in the bush to stand silently outside his home, without eating or drinking for two days, before dispersing back into the bush.

For Lawrence Anthony, to begin living in a world of savannah, or deep forest, populated with wildebeest, impala, cape buffalo, rhinoceros, and above all elephants was an abrupt change of life from the money world of board rooms, power lunches, and urban distraction. To try collapsing more than ten years of such a life into the neat words of an obituary can't even begin sampling the story.

Through his early negotiations with his adoptive elephant herd, Lawrence Anthony was to discover how willful wild elephants could be. The herd consisted of a matriarch, who had just seen her own mother culled, and six other individuals, all related, all traumatized by their recent experience of seeing members of their close family shot. No sooner had he corralled them in a *boma* designed to contain them until such time as they became habituated to their new home than they broke free, trying to return to their old stomping grounds in the far distant north. Repeatedly and with great difficulty they had to be re-captured.

As a last resort, Anthony tried camping outside their corral, day after day, night after night to make his presence known to them at all times, neither imposing himself on them, nor completely ignoring them. Every morning *at exactly 4:45*, the herd lined up at the electric fence ready to break out. The matriarch glared at him with murderous eyes. Every morning Anthony spoke to them in a gentle voice, addressing the matriarch directly: "Nana, you live here now. Everything will be safe for you here." By the third week Nana was still lining up with the herd behind her, ready to break out. "Don't do it, Nana," Anthony urged in a calm voice, "don't do it. This is your home now." As Anthony describes it, "Then something happened between Nana and me...." It was a look—an energy—that passed between them. I like to think it was the very same look that passed between five-year-old Marina Chapman and that silver capuchin patriarch in the far distant jungle bordering Venezuela and Colombia many years before.

Nana turned, and leading her herd, she retreated into the heart of the *boma*, signaling to Anthony they had now reached an "agreement," and that it was now time to set them free. Once liberated, they never again tried to break through the outer barriers surrounding the vast expanse of Thula Thula. But when, some years later, Anthony corralled a herd of antelope he intended to transport to another game reserve, Nana, who must have remembered the anguish of her own captivity, returned to the corral during the night, broke down the fence, and set the whole herd free.

Over the many subsequent years the herd roamed their new home and bore their young, Anthony continued to be amazed at what he recognized as their sense of fairness and their remarkable intelligence. When the matriarch became blind in one eye and was no longer able to see in the dark, her daughter, Frankie, led the herd at night, ceding daylight leadership back to the matriarch. When Anthony and his game keepers discovered an abandoned newly born calf in distress, and disregarded their own safety to return it to the herd, immediately its mother recognized it; the entire herd surrounded it, caressing its small, 240-pound body with their trunks. But Nana separated herself from the herd to face Anthony, standing for a long time silently. This now familiar gesture of hers had become her way of acknowledging his good intentions.

Throughout the time-span of which his three books mark the chronology, Lawrence Anthony rues the awkwardness of using English to talk to elephants. He acknowledges that, after all, elephants, like Jesus, don't speak English, much as some of the Christian world might prefer to imagine. From the beginning, Anthony repeatedly emphasizes that in his own mind, it is the tone in which he speaks—or shouts—that conveys meaning much more than the mere awkwardness of words. It comes from the total body-as-instrument. But the motivating energy comes from the psyche, and that seems to be the territory that requires further examination because some of the gifts-to-intuit belonging to such animals as whales and elephants reside in the physical body of which the cognitive brain is but a part.

There are many ways to send—and receive—messages, and these animals are among those who suggest that some of these ways may no longer be available to most of us as the "evolved" species we like to imagine ourselves to be. The recognition by elephants of the presence of a familiar human, even after a lapse of years, is a story repeatedly told. I know, for example, of someone who in his youth had spent a great deal of time with a particular favored elephant at the Berlin Zoo. At war's end, after the passage of many years, he returned to pay a visit. No sooner past the turnstiles, he heard the trumpeting of his favorite elephant who had already recognized him from the elephant house far distant from the gate.

But recognition by humans is a much rarer story. Over time, as Thula Thula's elephant herd multiplied, the growing number of unruly juvenile males had Anthony worried. He realized he would have to import a mature bull to socialize them. He chose a bull elephant, Gobisa by name, and he sent for an old gamekeeper he'd heard about, whose lifetime of bush lore qualified him for the job. Katcheni showed up barely a day after. "Elephants have a very strong spirit, and their spirit will find your spirit," he announced. "Gobisa knows I am here; he knew when I arrived, and I, too, I know where he is hiding." Although Katcheni had no previous knowledge of Thula Thula's terrain, he described in detail the ravine deep in the bush where he knew a homesick Gobisa must be sulking.

18. Big Spirit Mind

Anthony's story is one of immense effort and hard won gains learning the language of the landscape and of the huge animals living in it. There are no dictionaries—as yet—keyed to the language of elephants. (Katy Payne and her colleagues are working to develop one, but already in its inception, it seems to carry some of the misassumptions of anthropomorphism.) Like the true languages of animals anywhere, it has to be learned with great difficulty, by trial and at times life-risking error, one encounter at a time. For this, some humility is required, and a willingness to abandon years of absolute certainties, among them the mythos of species superiority. And if there is any doubt, the bulk—the menace—of a 5,000-pound wild animal whose hulk obliterates the light of the sun is there to remind where the terms must be set. Not only does it require a reordering of priorities, it requires "African time," unwinding of the industrialized speed-up, leaving behind the tyranny of the timepiece to orient oneself to the timing of sunlight, to the slow spread of shadow and light on the landscape. Anthony's initial daily encounters with the herd brought him to a deep understanding that if elephants are not approached on their own terms, efforts to acclimate them to a new range miles distant from the landscape in which they originally foraged would prove futile. Already during the first days of highly dangerous encounters he learned that nothing could be taken for granted. He was quickly disabused of the notion that in those initial negotiations he was in any way the master, or that be belonged to a somehow superior species. At the same time, he saw clearly that under the guidance of their matriarch, the elephants would meet him on their own terms and in their own good time. In the world of *homo sapiens*, we might distill from such encounters meanings of respect, of dignity, and perhaps above all, of the very deep listening without which there can be no meaningful interspecies—or for that matter infraspecies—communication. And we might possibly begin to question the efficacy of spoken language itself as the best possible vehicle.

Anthony was to use this awareness to remarkable advantage in the political arena of the day. Some months before his death, he learned through a reporter friend that the deep bush bordering Sudan and Uganda had become home to a barely surviving herd of northern white rhino, its number so reduced by the depredations of poachers bootlegging their horns for resale in Asian countries revering its aphrodisiac properties, it was barely sufficient to guarantee the gene pool. Their last retreat was in a remote game reserve called Garamba, deep in bush territory under the control of the Lords Resistance Army. Over the LRA's many years of marauding and inflicting atrocities against local people, Garamba's game wardens had become so fearful they refused to go out on patrol. Poachers had no problem infiltrating the game reserve and using it as their personal landing strip. From then on, Anthony became a man obsessed with a mission: saving the northern white rhino from extinction. Through highly placed political connections he had been able to enter Baghdad at the time of "shock and awe" when Baghdad became all but a fire storm, to save the 35 animals in the Baghdad zoo that had not already died of starvation, or been stolen and eaten for food. His negotiations with the Lords Resistance Army came about by a kind of magnificent indirection; but without "big spirit mind," it is doubtful he could ever have dreamed up anything to match it. After trying to leap the procedural hurdles erected by an African bureaucracy schooled to a fine point by its former colonialist masters, he finally realized that the only recourse left to him was negotiating directly with the LRA guerillas who controlled the area bordering the game reserve.

No one had ever met these fearsome guerillas in their stronghold deep in the bush, let alone talked to them directly. Faced with trying to make contact with people who occupied a vast and undeveloped territory deep in Africa's heart, and who—with good reason—had lost all ability to trust, Anthony flew via Nairobi to Juba, Sudan's capital, where actual peace talks were in progress between the warring parties of the Ugandan Civil War. Accompanied by Julie, the reporter friend who first brought the rhino's looming extinction to his attention, and her husband Christopher, the three soon discovered they were embarked on a wild goose chase with roadblocks at every turn. But Anthony, perhaps because he had never graduated from high school and had not exactly taken to the ways in which "normal" folks construe the world, cajoled customs officials, badgering them into exhausted submission. He bribed an AK-47-wielding tough guy in the Nairobi airport to get his crew past customs, and, once arrived in Juba, caught the rare taxi by waving $100 against the windshield. Once he was able to discover from the cabbie where they were taking place, he crashed the peace talks by claiming all three were a television crew (his companions' cameras and press credentials stood them in good stead), only to sit around two days trying to make face-to-face contact with the LRA. As a desperate last resort, he introduced himself directly to a tight huddle of their representatives—only to be stonewalled by complete and utter silence. But after a few days, a casual meeting in the conference garden finally set up the diplomatic conditions, which brought him in contact with the LRA's diplomatic arm.

From them he learned that, although they had repeatedly offered to lay down their arms, the prospect of peace was extremely unlikely as long as the U.S. wanted to keep Museveni in power as president of Uganda. And for Museveni himself, the conflict provided his meal ticket for continued U.S. aid. But nonetheless the LRA were willing to hear Anthony out and to entertain his proposal for saving the few remaining northern whites from extinction. That the Acholi people, of which the LRA is exclusively composed, revered the rhino as their totem certainly helped to grease the skids.

In these negotiations, Anthony brought to bear everything he had learned from elephants: persistence and deep respect from days of confronting angry rogue animals each dawn at precisely 4:45, and most of all faith that eventually, with patience and persistence, his good intentions would be recognized and ultimately the LRA would come to trust him. And indeed, after several days spent vetting him and assessing his motives, the LRA spokesperson OK'd him: "We can see that you are a man of the animals." Observes Anthony: "In the West, that analogy may mean you're a bit different. But in Africa it is an interesting compliment. It means you are unlike others in a *spiritual* sense [itals added]: that you are somehow part of the animal kingdom and not entirely of the world of humans…. It also meant that I had no financial, political, or military agendas."

Once the LRA was satisfied, they agreed to pull their warriors away from the warden's camp at Garamba game reserve; they promised not to interfere with the rangers' patrols; they would prevent the killing of any rhinos by poachers; and they would keep on the lookout for any rhinos they might find in the bush and report back to Anthony. It became the *very first treaty* of its kind ever to be signed in the context of any peace talks.*

---

* Recent reports from Garamba indicate that as of June, 2014 it had become open season with 68 elephants killed by poachers within two months.

Ultimately, the LRA promised to lay down their arms, and they kept their promise, and because a truce went into effect, two million Acholi people, who had been rounded up by Museveni and confined to concentration camps where they were forced to live—and die—in horrific conditions, were allowed to return home. Conclusions are never perfect, but conditions that allow two million refugees to return to their homes after years of war amount to a human victory. And perhaps the reversal initially came about because a man had learned listening and trusting from elephants.

Besides being page-turners, both *The Elephant Whisperer* and its sequel, *The Last Rhino,* can be studied as primers, basic lessons in how better to grasp our place in the world as members of the human species, and how it might be possible to live here more sustainably, and in a state, if not of outright happiness, at least with the feeling of wellbeing that comes from a sense of connectedness to living things.

Which raises the question: Were such ways of communicating perhaps available to *us* once in the very remote prehistoric past, in the time when we were already primates but not quite yet fully human (if indeed we are)? And if they were available to us in the past, might they be accessible once again? And if they were to become accessible, what ends might they serve?

The answers—at least as of now—must remain speculative at best. But the arc of Lawrence Anthony's life may provide some kind of window to understanding that the human mind as it encounters the elephant-mind or the whale-mind may be far more limited in its capacities than we might care to imagine; it suggests that some of these extra-human capabilities can be approached in terms not yet named or defined by "science" as accepted norms of communication; and that these same, unnamed capabilities can extend themselves into the world of nearly intractable human conflict to work, if not towards total resolution, at least to partial remediation—what positivists like to call "a first step." Because without that first step, there is no peace, there is no possibility of peace; the darkness of a world in conflagration descends once more, as exemplified by Lawrence Anthony's personal, face-to-face contact with Joseph Kony and the commanders of the notorious Lords Resistance Army.

The Thula Thula elephants had consistently emerged from the bush to stand by the reserve gates whenever Anthony came home from his many trips. They always seemed to know the exact hour of his return. It is debatable whether the reason they came out of the bush at the time of his death 800 miles away in Johannesburg was to mark his passing. They may very well have come—after an absence of some two years—because they sensed he was coming home. But not to eat and not to drink for two whole days before they finally dispersed to return to the bush—for that there is no known explanation.

Known in the received sense that humans know everything.

19. Insufficient Elephants

The biggest problem we face is a philosophical one:
understanding that this civilization is already dead.

—Roy Scranton

Thirty-five thousand (that's 35,000) elephants were killed by poachers in 2013. "It makes me so angry, I want to get a gun," remarks a young man attending a recent Buddhist gathering. A small laugh escapes from me unbidden. Who is this young man, I wonder? And how will he get his gun? Overcome his presumably Buddhist reluctance to shoot anything? It might be done. Where would he go to get that gun? Overcome an ingrained habit to find a gun shop, or a gun fair? Plunk down his money? It might be done. Would he need to fly to Uganda, perhaps? Plunk down plenty lucre for an airline ticket? It might be done. Who will he have to shoot? The poacher? Not easy. Many poachers like helicopters that fly low, AK-47s and other impressive caliber weapons. But it could be done—with some inconvenience, perhaps. But who would he be shooting? A starving African looking for bush meat? (Yes, hungry people eat elephant meat. Millennia ago they ate human meat as well—and it could be said they still do—in acceptable war-making fashion.) Or an insurgent who hopes to fund an insurrection through the highly profitable ivory trade, the very kind of insurgent attempting to overthrow the murderous government of Museveni, perhaps? Shoot Museveni? Hard to do with all that protection money dictators like to throw around. But who is propping up Museveni, keeping him in power? The United States, bent on plundering Africa's natural resources, and rich enough to buy its dictators by the barrel. Shoot the Secretary of State? Congress? The President? The shadow government? Aw, shucks, how about the carvers of ivory? Easier perhaps. But the carver works in a sweat shop and has a family of 16 all living under one roof to feed. How about the ivory wholesalers, and folks who make collecting ivory a dedication? Hard to smoke them out in their Beijing and Hong Kong high rises. And anyway, after gun acquisition and transportation there's no budget left for all the ammunition he would need. Resisting the imperial aspirations of one's own government may be the more economical solution. Expenses can be held at a minimum: fines, imprisonment for non-violent civil disobedience. But the work is harder, longer hours are required, a ferocious level of dedication, a life-time commitment really. The pay is poor, the hours long. It's steady work, but not any work for sissies. Or he might simply conclude there are too many people, especially needy people, and insufficient elephants, and go home.

Three themes unite Nollman, Anthony, and Payne, whose work is described here. All are working and writing "outside their expertise," that is, none of them are trained as naturalists or animal "experts." Two of them are autodidacts. Of the three, one of them never graduated from high school. And each one has either an active or passive relationship with music. From this we might deduce further that a relationship to music might make of one a more careful listener. It also speaks to the ineffability of music, and of music as a unifying language, perhaps because of its very ineffability, ineffable in the sense that it is an expression, like that of sign language, that bypasses spoken words and any need of them. Writes Katy Payne:

> Just being silent is a most wonderful way to open up to what is really there. I see my responsibility, if I have one, as being to listen. My sense is that community responsibility, when it's managed well, results in peace. And peace benefits everyone. That taking care of someone or something to which you are not immediately genetically related pays you back in other dimensions, and the payback is part of your wellbeing. Compassion is useful and beneficial for all....
>
> My church is outdoors mostly. What's sacred to me is this planet we live on. It's been here for more than 4 billion years. Life has been on it only for 3 billion years. Life as we know it, you know, for a very short time. It's the only planet where life has been found. And that, to me, I think, is ultimately sacred....

Given the frightful impasse in which the planet now finds itself, it is perhaps time to defrock the left-brain priesthood of people we should no longer look to as "experts," scientific and otherwise, and to forsake our own addiction to bowing down to them. It also makes a strong case that there is something deeply flawed with what we like to call "education," a system that turns away many an original mind to seek its life's nourishment elsewhere. Perhaps it suggests that the time has come to learn to sing. Writes Lawrence Anthony: "I have never understood the saying, 'To think outside the box.' Why would anyone sit inside of a box and then think outside of it. Rather just get out of the box."

20. Wolf Cries

There is nothing like the whip of fear to lash men into a fury of destruction. Whenever and wherever men have engaged in the mindless slaughter of animals (including other men) they have often attempted to justify their acts by attributing the most vicious or revolting qualities to those they would destroy; and the less reason there is for the slaughter, the greater the campaign of vilification.

—Farley Mowat in *Never Cry Wolf*

Quite recently my habit of trolling bookshelves in unfamiliar places yielded a book whose details had long faded into the remote past, but whose impression has never quite left me since first reading it some fifty years ago. *Never Cry Wolf,* a study of the habits of the arctic wolf, is graced with deep humility and saving humor. Commissioned in the 1950s by the Ottawa government to investigate how wolves must be the culprits responsible for decimating a caribou population from 4 million in 1930 to fewer than 170,000 by 1963, field biologist Farley Mowat set out for the tundra with a set of government instructions that might have been drawn up by a functionary of Kafka's *Castle* in collaboration with a Japanese Mikado, and enough field supplies to crash a bush plane.

Received notions tend to die hard and, freshly arrived in the Keewatin Barrens, Mowat's were no exception—but describing himself as "cleansed and spiritually purified" by a night of nursing a bottle of grain alcohol, he determined to open his mind to the lupine world, learning to see the wolves, not for what the ranchers and hunters backed by the sclerotic weight of the Ottawa government were claiming them to be, but for what they were. Gifted with a good pair of eyes, a decent telescope, and his scientific training, Mowat was able to camp and work in the Barrens throughout the temperate months where he observed a wolf den sheltering three adult wolves and a litter of pups, and documented their activities day-to-day.

With his six-inch paw print, the alpha male was larger than the female and must have weighed some 250 pounds. Mowat named him George for his regal qualities. The female—whom Mowat named Angeline in keeping with her good nature—and the alpha male formed a breeding pair. Although not at first apparent, the role of the third adult male—whom Mowat named Albert—became clear some time later when, after a strenuous hour of roughhousing and badgering by her pups, Angeline's howl of dismay was such that Albert immediately took over the role of babysitter, allowing himself to be tormented by ear pulling and biting, and other baby lupine pleasures. Later on, as the pups became weaned, his role expanded to staying with them overnight, allowing Angeline to resume hunting with her mate.

Arctic wolves require an area of some 300 square miles to sustain their life by hunting. They mark their boundaries much as dogs do to discourage intruders. Hunting is preceded by a period of apparent restlessness followed by several minutes during which they form a circle and howl in unison—a possible example of ritual as practiced by animals. (Another possibility is that circle-howling represents a threat or perhaps a courtesy "agreement" whereby one species may warn other species the hunt is about to begin.)

Through careful observation of their hunting habits, Mowat discovered that, far from decimating caribou herds, individuals in the Keewatin Barrens den subsisted on a diet of arctic mice! As soon as the pups were weaned, Angeline moved them to a naturally enclosed "nursery" area where all three adults cooperated to teach them mouse-hunting skills.

Mowat discovered wolves use an almost unlimited variety of hunting strategies. Catching mice, their main staple, involved a simple leap and pounce. To trap fresh-water fish, wolves immersed themselves nearly up to their bellies and kicked their legs up to raise great splashes of water, driving the fish upstream into increasingly narrow river channels until they were corralled. Mowat himself borrowed this technique to tasty advantage—a present-day example of human learning from animals.

A large group of wolves sometimes forms a *battue,* in which one team harries the prey towards a second team, which captures and kills it. Wolves take only what they need. If a larger kill is brought to the den, the wolves take the next day off, happy to loaf and sleep in the sun. In one of those calm intervals when the hunt produced a surplus of food, Mowat watched Albert collapse in a state of near exhaustion while George, assuring himself that Albert had gone sound asleep, slowly crept up on him and pounced with all his weight. An outraged Albert gave chase and soon what started out as a practical joke turned into a game of tag.

Mowat describes a rich vocabulary of lupine social interactions. Angelina and George often engaged in mock tag and combat, which Angeline followed by effusive signs of affection, embracing him with her forepaws and licking the forbearing George's face. Angelina always waited expectantly for him to return from the hunt, and greeted him and Albert with elaborate expressions of joy.

When bachelor Albert fell in love with Kooa, a Huskie bitch who had gone into heat, Mowat was able to observe a very nuanced wolf courtship.

> I do not know how long Albert had been celibate, but it had clearly been too long.... When he was within ten feet of Kooa, he stopped dead in his tracks, lowered his great head, and turned into a buffoon. It was an embarrassing spectacle. He...began to whine in a wheedling falsetto, which would have sounded disgusting [even] coming from a Pekinese. With a half snarl, Kooa backed away from Albert as far as her chain would permit. This sent Albert into a frenzy of abasement. Belly to earth he began to grovel toward her while his grimace widened into an expression of sheer idiocy. [Then he] shifted gears with bewildering rapidity. Scrambling to his feet he suddenly became the lordly male. His ruff expanded until it made a huge silvery aura framing his face.

His tail rose until it was as high and almost as tightly curled as a true Husky's. Then pace by delicate pace, he closed the gap. Kooa was no longer in doubt. This was something she could understand.

With arctic wolves, estrus lasts a bare three weeks, but they have developed various strategies to control overpopulation. For one thing, litter size will depend on food availability. When food is plentiful, a litter might number up to eight pups, but when food is scarce, the litter size might fall to one or two. Females do not breed until the age of two, and males wait until they reach three. If a nursing female is shot or poisoned while there are pups in the den, the bereaved male will seek out a male wolf in another territory to help him carry the pups to a new den where a nursing female will accept and treat them as her own. Wolves mate for life but unavailability of a suitable den often prevents them. Much as they might be driven to start a family, often there is not enough hunting territory available to provide the wherewithal for every bitch to produce a litter.

If such controlling factors were not to operate, the population would become so numerous that it would become diseased or perish of starvation. Just recently, wolf conservation officials in Yellowstone, concerned that the mate of a nursing mother had been killed by hunters, rounded up the mother and her pups, and provided food for them over several months in an acclimation pen. But they feared she would have difficulty caring for the pups once they were returned to the wild. The day of their release, a bachelor wolf living in a far distant part of the park happened to show up outside the pen just in time to form a new family unit.

Keen as Mowat seems to have been to see and describe what he saw of wolf social behavior, he had to wait for Ootek, an Inuit shaman, to appear on the scene to help him fathom the complexities of actual wolf language. The Inuit have been living with wolves for hundreds of years, in much the same way as Aborigines relate to dolphins. Ootek's nephew, who spoke English, explained that the wolves not only were able to communicate over long distances, but that they could talk, certainly as well as he did. He assured

Mowat that although he could neither hear all their sounds nor understand most of them, some Inuit, such as his uncle Ootek in particular, could hear and understand so well, that—his lack of English fluency notwithstanding!—he could actually converse with them.

Wolves make use of their own bush telegraph. Each den exists at a remove of at least 17 linear miles from the neighboring den's hunting territory. Given such vast distances, Mowat cites many examples of Ootek's ability to hear and interpret a wolf's howls. On one occasion, Ootek heard George responding to a miles-distant howl coming from the neighboring territory. From its timbre he recognized that the neighbor's howl had been passed along from an even more remote territory to the north, and that it was announcing that caribou had begun to migrate into the far-distant wolf's territory. But even before hearing Ootek's interpretation of what he heard, Ootek's nephew was already packing up his sled and heading north to hunt the deer.

Once when Mowat remained utterly baffled by what Ootek was trying to tell him, Ootek finally gave up and took off in frustration only to return some time later in the company of three friends. Later Ootek's nephew explained to Mowat that from the timbre of George's howl, Ootek could tell that Inuit hunters were passing through the adjacent territory and, disgusted by Mowat's evident obtuseness, abruptly took off to intercept his friends.

Whenever George returned to the den after a night out hunting, Angelina waited patiently for his return. On one occasion, her repeated trips to the crest of the hill to watch went unrewarded. After some time, Ootek heard a howl from a distant territory, yet he was unable to make Mowat understand what exactly he had heard. He ventured back to his nephew's cabin for a nap. Toward noon, Mowat observed an exhausted George returning from the hunt. Once awakened from his nap, and with his nephew back in the cabin to translate, Ootek was able to explain what he had been trying to convey earlier.

"Ootek says that wolf you call George, he send a message to his wife," Ootek's nephew told Mowat. "Ootek hear it good. He tell his wife the hunting is pretty bad and he going to stay out longer. Maybe not get home until the middle of the day." Mowat had in fact noted the time of George's return. It clocked in at exactly 17 minutes after noon.

Despite his careful observation and documentation of wolf culture and wolf prey, Mowat's conclusion is not optimistic:

> During the winter of 1958-59, the Canadian Wildlife Service, in pursuance of its continuing policy of wolf control, employed several predator control officers to patrol the Keewatin Barrens in ski-equipped aircraft for the purpose of setting out poison bait stations.... In early May of 1959, one of them landed in the [den] vicinity for some hours and placed a number of cyanide "wolf getters" in appropriate places near the den, which, so he ascertained, was occupied. He also spread a number of strychnine-treated baits in the vicinity.... He was unable to return at a later date to check on this control station, because of the early onset of the spring thaws.... It is not known what results were obtained.

Since then, Man's relationship to wolves has undergone little change perhaps because somewhere in his buried memory lurks the frustration of having failed to colonize wolves into submissive dogs. In the September/October 2013 issue of *Orion Magazine* Jon Donnelly writes:

> [After] the Fed recently lifted protections, nearly 1,200 wolves out of a population of almost 2,000 in Wyoming, Montana, and Idaho have been slain by hunters and trappers. Hunters in Minnesota and Wisconsin, home to more than 4,000 wolves, have killed nearly 500 since hunts were sanctioned. Michigan became the sixth state to approve wolf hunting. Guns, crossbows, and foot traps are all permitted. It's scheduled to take place during the winter holiday season.

And on February 28, 2014, the Idaho Department of Fish and Game announced that, working together with Wildlife "Services," they succeeded in gunning down twenty-three wolves from a helicopter in Idaho's Lolo elk zone near the Idaho/Montana border. Presumably wolves are not considered game animals. The "services" attributed their burning need to kill them to boost the elk "harvest," despite evidence from independent peer reviewers that habitat loss, not predators, is the major factor in local elk herd decline.

Warfare between men and wolves continues to be appallingly asymmetric. Still, Jim Nollman cites one reputed instance early in the 20th century when a Montana wolf collected a pile of wolf traps. Carefully balancing on it, he defecated.

21. A Dream Dreaming Us: The Real People

Of all places, I first came across Laurens van der Post's writing in Belgrade, Yugoslavia, where I had gone to attend the BITEF theater festival of 1974. Organizers of the festival had been reading the paperback edition of *The Lost World of the Kalahari*, which, luckily enough, eventually fell to me as the next in line. Published in 1958, five years before *Never Cry Wolf*, it came to haunt my imagination, although its details had faded with time.

Revisiting it in 2013 has left a somewhat altered impression. This time I was struck by the book's overlong emphasis on the expedition, led by van der Post, a white European, whose Afrikaans sensibilities were shaped from early childhood by the immense skies of Africa, and by one of his parent's aging menservants who fired his child's imagination with intimations of another Way.

Under contract to the BBC, van der Post's expedition not only occupies itself with filming but with careful descriptive documentation. Little is said of the San, commonly referred to as the Bushmen of the Kalahari Desert or, variously, the !Kung, !Kung-San, or Ju/'hoansi, until the last sixty pages of the 280-page work. But, despite tedious dissention among the European expedition's participants that impedes their journey at every turn, the last sixty pages reward the reader with a startling glimpse of that borderland where van der Post's 1950s world, in all its ignorant forgetfulness makes brief and poignant contact with people living as our ancestors must have lived more than 30,000 years ago—a living fossil reminder to us still in the present day.

Van der Post describes the San as bound by almost no possessions, the most valued being the mortar and pestle painstakingly fashioned by hand out of ironwood that each woman carries on her back during the long seasonal migrations required for survival in a landscape described as "a world so harsh that even the greediest among us had shunned it"—a landscape that winnows the older generation as relentlessly as the Inuit who leave their aged behind to succumb to the arctic snows. He describes their bee-hive-shaped huts, so cunningly designed as to be barely visible, even in the midst of such sparse landscapes. Their social organization as he describes it seems to be variously either matrilineal or patrilineal. According to their marriage customs, young brides return to live and sleep in their maternal home during the period in which they become more familiar with their husbands. Often the couple will come to live in the maternal group where the young bride benefits from the support of other women in her clan. In times of great thirst, women cease to menstruate, but if, in such a period a child is born, the women of the group—those most attached to children—take the child "before its mother's heart learns to cry for it," to expose and end its life. The practice extends to children born handicapped, and because women carry a child over four thousand miles of foraging until, at the age of four, it no longer nurses and can walk by itself, one twin of two is always sacrificed.

Ancient Bushman sites, found mostly in caves and mountain hollows, depict in breathtaking color the figures of humans and animals still held dear and sacred to the San. But, by the 1950s, pictorial art is no longer present in Bushman life as van der Post describes it. When he shows the members of a small settlement images he has taken of such sites, the younger generation views them dispassionately; but when he shows such images to the truly old, they break down weeping.

With the help of a native shaman and an expert San tracker, van der Post's expedition sets out to find Tsodilo (meaning
"slippery") Hills, a deeply concealed place alive with the varicol-
ored rock paintings for which the ancient San were once noted
and where they gather each year for their yearly spring coming
together. But despite his empathetic sensibilities, van der Post is
not yet prepared to recognize the import of the shaman's conditions that if he is to lead all twenty-eight men, white and native, there must be no more dissension amongst the expedition's
leaders, and no shooting or killing of any kind along the way.
Unaware of the shaman's strictures, van der Post's companions
continue to shoot game, as they have throughout the journey,
providing food without which they believe the expedition cannot proceed.

From the outset, the group encounters mysterious and unexplained difficulties: their camp at the foot of Tsodilo Hills is attacked every dawn by swarms of bees; despite replacement by new
magazines, film cameras repeatedly and consistently break down;
and when the shaman kneels to pray he is mysteriously knocked
over, nearly falling to his death. But worst of all, because of delays
brought about by their dissension, the expedition arrives only to
find the San have broken camp and left.

"The spirits of the hills are not what they were," laments the
shaman. And, turning to van der Post, "they are losing their power.
Ten years ago they would have killed you for coming to them [as
you have]."

Van der Post realizes that forgetting to share the shaman's
conditions with the others must be at the root of their various
misfortunes. But the shaman assures him that things will return to
normal once van der Post writes a letter of apology to the spirits
of the hills, and puts it in a bottle to be buried under the sand.
And indeed for the first time since their arrival, next morning the
bees fail to visit, the cameras work, and the Land Rovers start
up without a hitch. But nonetheless, van der Post is constrained
to observe: "I have always had a profound respect for aboriginal
superstition, not as formulations of literal truth, but as a way of

keeping the human spirit obedient to aspects of reality that are beyond rational articulation."

Because of their protracted setbacks and delays, van der Post opts to curtail the expedition's original schedule and directly seek the place his tracker remembers from his childhood where, in the driest months of thirst, the Bushmen sink five-foot-deep sip wells to suck water from beneath the desert sands, a secret shared only with other members of their tribe. It is the tracker who first spots one of the men who knows how to "sip the sand for water." From the moment the expedition's members hear the traditional San greeting, "Good day. I have been dead, but now that you have come, I live again," matters take a turn for the better. Their greeter turns out to be a man named Nxou (meaning "food bowl"), the group's young headman-to-be, and true to his name's promise, a superb hunter.

Under his guidance, all the expedition members join in helping the men of the small settlement hunt for an eland, that most prized of hunting prey. From early morning to mid afternoon, the San follow the tracks of some fifty eland, trotting in pursuit. The members of the expedition follow the hunters in their Land Rovers, but when at last the San spot the herd, they pursue them at such speed that the Land Rovers can barely manage to keep up. At one point Nxou leaps over a cobra, hood extended, ready to strike, without even a backward glance. The chase continues for twelve miles, the San running so fast they actually pass out of view. At last, the runners corner the huge bull they have previously managed to wound, but, although already wounded, it continues holding its head high, looking steadily at the hunters closing in on it with their spears. They drive their spears straight into its heart, but even then, the great animal won't die until van der Post puts a bullet through its head. Without a pause for rest the San lose no time skinning the kill.

Extraordinary in itself, the account of the hunt is nothing compared to the cultural surprise waiting for the Europeans at day's end. Nxou explains that from the beginning, no Bushman ever kills an eland without thanking it by returning home to dance. Van der Post wonders out loud what the little group back home by the sip wells will say when they learn the hunters have successfully killed an eland. "They already know," is the reply. They know "by wire," the guide explains, tapping his chest. "We Bushmen have a 'wire' here that brings us news." Although the hunters have ranged some fifty miles over the desert's many twists and turns, they still know home's exact location. And indeed, as they approach, they hear others of the group welcoming them in the far distance by singing the song they call "The Eland Song."

Van der Post reports the San way of life as being one rich with music, sung and played on some of the earliest instruments known to humans. Dancing is an integral part of the San communal way of life. One of their dances commemorates a long-forgotten war. Two teams of dancers face one another perhaps fifteen yards apart but on their knees, taunting and challenging each other. They accompany their taunts with mock spear thrusts, and twisting and turning in mimed evasive action, with gestures of the wounded and dying, still executed on their knees. The story goes that, although the original war was fought with apparent savagery, unlike the wars of Europeans, it was followed by such shared revulsion at its cruelty, they resolved never again to let such a thing happen. From then on, the San have divided the desert into two zones, promising never to cross the dividing line between them, and still now, they never cross it. Superb naturalists, the San still recognize markers all over the landscape that indicate the line's strict demarcations, paralleling the kind of "arrangement" also observed by wolves and marine animals.

Even more extraordinary is van der Post's description of the Rain Dance. At the first peel of distant thunder that follows the onslaught of the great and scorching heat of summer, the entire small community bursts into dance. Writes van der Post, "This music was rich, varied, tender and filled with unworldly longing. It had a curious weave and rhythm to it, some deep-river movement of life, turning and twisting, swirling and eddying back upon itself in order to round some invisible objects in its profound bed as it swept on to the sea."

It is a dance that continues into the evening. Towards nightfall, taking great pains to use a minimum of timber, the San light a fire. The men form a ring around it, miming in their dance the first Bushman soul setting out in darkness to look for fuel for the fire; they call upon the sun, moon and stars to give them fire. At the climax of the dance, one man breaks free to scoop up a handful of burning coals, attempting to swallow them whole. Then almost at midnight an elder uncle suddenly "finds" it and when he kneels down beside it, the singing finally dies away in one last sob. He stoops to pick up the coals in his bare hands and scatters them far and wide for all the world to share. At that moment, the rain begins to fall.

Once they had shared their rain dance with the Europeans, the San felt free at last to impart their traditional myths and legends and Nxou's belief that there is "a dream dreaming us." Over an entire day, and several days following, they revealed their oldest stories, from creation to the last defeat of the Bushman spirit when their ancestors were torn apart from those others of the human race and expelled into the desert's harsh and unforgiving wastes, where only the young and fit survive.

> A day will come when [the old] can't go on. Then, weeping bitterly, all will gather round them. They'll give them all the food and water they can spare. They'll build a thick shelter of thorn to protect them against wild animals. Still weeping, the rest of the band, like the life that asks it of them, will move on. It has always been like that…for those who survive the hazards of the desert to grow truly old. Sooner or later, probably before their water or food is finished, a leopard, but more commonly a hyena, will break through and eat them.

Some time later, reviewing his experience, van der Post concludes:

> [I felt our] encounter had for a moment made me immediate, and had, all too briefly, closed a dark time-gap in myself. We have forgotten the importance of being truly and openly primitive. We have forgotten the art of our legitimate

beginnings. We no longer know how to close the gap between the far past and the immediate present in ourselves.... Of all the nostalgias that haunt the human heart the greatest of them all, for me, is an everlasting longing to bring what is youngest home to what is oldest in us all."

Although van der Post makes no mention of their language, the San speak !Kung, (the ! symbol stands for a particular click sound), the first variant of the three "click" languages in the group known as Khoisan, so named and classified by Joseph Greenberg, a pioneer of world linguistics, as being the earliest language group spoken by humankind.

Greenberg seems to be reviled by most historical linguists because of his unorthodox methods, but "his classification of the Khoisan languages seems a stroke of genius in light of a surprising new link that has now emerged among them," according to Nicholas Wade writing in *Before the Dawn*.

That link lies at the intersection of historical linguistics and the study of genetics. The San or !Kung show several lineages of mitochondrial DNA, but the main one forms the first branch of L1, defined as the oldest of the three divisions of the human mitochondrial tree. Their mitochondrial DNA shows them to be one of the two most ancient populations in the world. (The others are the speakers of Hadza, also a "click" language). Geneticist Douglas Wallace of UC-Irvine notes that the division "is positioned at the deepest root of the African phylogenetic tree, suggesting the !Kung-San split off from the ancestral population at between 60,000 and 90,000 years ago and have remained distinct as a population ever since. Astronomical references suggest that their historic memory reverts at least that far. (See Section 41.)

As hunter-gatherers, the !Kung-San have managed to preserve their isolation from other populations for millennia. Archeologists believe that in Paleolithic times, the San occupied the entire eastern half of Africa as far north as the Red Sea and Ethiopia where in the present day two tribes, the Amara and the Oromo, show a small proportion of Y chromosomes belonging to the first branch of the Y–chromosome family tree, a branch rare in Africa except among the !Kung-San, where 44 percent carry it. (The mitochondrial DNA of women of the Amara and Oromo also indicates that Ethiopia is probably the place from which the first modern humans may have left Africa approximately 50,000 years ago.)

In contrast to Laurens van der Post, Wade, writing some fifty years later, paints a far less bucolic picture of the San. Largely based on a Harvard study conducted twenty years later, in 1970, he describes the San as strictly egalitarian, with no governing authority other than personal persuasion. Individuals must resolve by themselves or with the help of kin such disagreements that they can't walk away from, "preventing them as a society from growing beyond a certain level of either size or complexity." (Wade's governing principle here seems to be an imperative for growth.) According to this study, San rock art depicts a warlike past, anticipating a present-day homicide rate of 29.3 per 100,000 person-years, more than three times that of the United States.

But there is cause to suppose that ultimately, beauty rests in the eye of whoever happens to be watching. Compared to Wade's, the account of Elizabeth Marshall Thomas, who spent her girlhood years in the Kalahari, breathes with a much deeper level of human understanding. Her views of the San were gathered over many years while she lived with her anthropologist parents in close proximity to the Nyae Nyae group of San, sharing much of their daily lives. Her account, *The Old Way*, affords a deeply empathetic albeit fiercely unsentimental view.

Marshall reports in troubling detail that nowadays the San are being crowded out of their territories by the encroachment of cattlemen and vacation resorts, and many of them are being forced to join money economies, whether as lowly underpaid hands or as allotment small farmers. Some try to survive living on the margins of resort areas where their desperate poverty is seen as an offence to more advantaged eyes.

Ironically, now that survival of the San way of life is very much in doubt, anthropologists are beginning to respect and use the name the !Kung-San still use to identify themselves, namely, the *Ju/'hoansi*, or the Real People. (The San identify unreal people

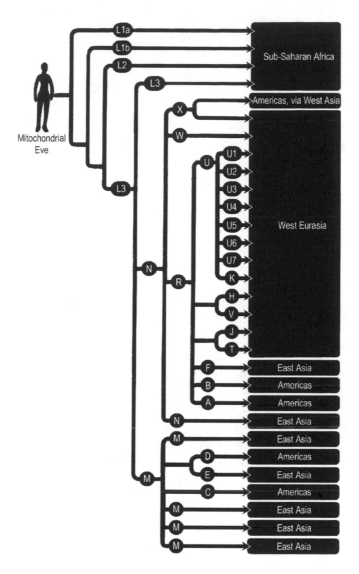

Figure 1. Mitochondrial DNA Family Tree. All men and women carry
the same mitochondrial DNA, derived from a mitochondrial Eve. The
single version of MDNA—inherited only through the female line—has
collected mutations over time and can be used to assign women to lineages. All sub-Saharan women belong to one of the first three branches
of MDNA (Lineages L1, L2, and L3). Europeans belong to Lineage
N. (Daughter lineages A,B,C,D, and X are of people who reached the
American hemispheres.)

as !ohm, a term, according to Wade, that "includes Europeans, predators, and other inedible beasts.") But, as Elizabeth Marshall Thomas explains, their name, which she spells as *Ju/wasi*, means much more. It means the "Clear People, the Worthwhile People, the People Who Have Left Their Weapons Somewhere Else, The Harmless People. *Ju*...means 'person' and */wa*...reflects the way the people live together and relate to one another...in the hand-holding chain that goes [far] back through time."

San Spirituality, by David Williams and David Pearce, sums it up:

> Since the 1950s [the time of van der Post's expedition], change has been rapid. The San...are no longer allowed to hunt the animals they once did and they have inevitably been caught up in the political changes that have taken place in Namibia and Botswana. They now have access to schools and hospitals, but poverty is their overwhelming lot. They manage to earn some money by making curios for tourists and by performing the medicine dance, but for the most part they live around small villages.... Tin shanties have started to take the place of traditional dwellings, and firearms are greatly coveted....Life in the Kalahari will never return to the sort of existence that [Elizabeth Marshall Thomas or for that matter Laurens van der Post] found.

This is a tragedy because theirs was a civilization which managed to live sustainably on the planet for at least 35,000 years.

Generally, when ungulates encounter carnivores, the results are almost invariably the same: those at the top of the food chain tend to win the encounter. But even in the world of animals, there are exceptions. In 2002, in Kenya's Samburu Game Reserve, a lioness came to the attention of park workers. She had adopted a baby oryx from its mother shortly after birth, having scared the mother away. The lioness became attached to the calf and protected it from attacks by leopards and cheetahs intent on having a suckling oryx for dinner, but exhausted from watching over it, she fell asleep only to discover upon awakening that a lion had pounced on it and dragged it away. The lioness was reported howling with grief, ranging over the game park, frantically looking for her foundling. One year later, park workers reported that she had tried to adopt six more oryx babies, releasing the last one only long enough to let its mother suckle it.

Whenever, throughout history, a gentler people come in contact with a people who are warlike, the results have usually been unfortunate for the gentler people. Happily history affords a few contrary examples that we would be well advised to study: the non-violent Mohandas Gandhi-led Salt March, which flummoxed British colonizers; and in Cochabamba, in more recent times, the indigenous protests led by Oscar Olivera against Aguas del Tunari, a consortium led by International Water Limited (England), Edison Utilities (Italy), Bechtel Enterprise Holdings (USA), and two Bolivian companies, which upturned the World Bank (USA) and ejected Aguas from Bolivia, Latin America's poorest country (see pp. 168ff).

22. Lily Mind

For millennia Chinese tradition held that at the age of five women of the privileged class must have their small feet broken in two, the extremities folded under the instep, and bound in strips of cloth. Having "lily feet" distinguished a woman who was wealthy enough to be able to depend on servants to carry her physically to the few places she was allowed to go.

For modern humans of European origin, the child-mind is as surely and cruelly bound as the feet of traditional privileged girl Chinese. The only difference is that the maiming is not always physically apparent because it is more predominantly of a psychic nature, and not visible to the naked eye. Yet, before the maiming, the child-mind is possessed of many of the gifts still preserved by many so-called "animals," and people dismissed as "primitive," and who historically were hunted down exactly as were animals.

From the time of our birth into the strata of existence we

call human life, and, as I will suggest, long before, we begin to receive cultural messages—call it imprinting—that domesticates our planetary nature bit by bit until we no longer have any sense of what endowments we might have lost along the way. Activist Webb Mealy tells the story of his then five-year-old daughter visiting Pauline, a pregnant friend. "Amber, do you know what Pauline has in her belly? A baby."

Muttered Amber, "No. Two."

And indeed, some months later Pauline gave birth to twins.

During my own childhood and well into adulthood, I had a recurring dream. From the dark night of space, a fiery object was hurtling out of the heavens toward me. I heard its drone approaching louder and louder. I knew with utter certainty that it was coming to explode my entire body into fiery fragments and—with that knowing—my body would be seized both inside and outside with a resonating concussion. Now that the terror of targeted assassination by drone warfare has entered the world of real, day-to-day existence, I ask myself if all these many dream images did not presage what would become one of the many horrors of our post-industrial life.

In 1940, sick with chicken pox, I remember having the most frightening nightmare of my life. It took place in an amphitheater familiar to me from childhood where, as part of a demonstration in child psychology, my mother had exposed me naked to an audience of adults. In the dream, from my place at the heart of the amphitheater, I could observe high up on its periphery a long assembly line of clanking parts, much like the Harlem shooting gallery where my father, compensating for my not having been born male, used to take me every Saturday to fire at the clay pigeons. In an upper corner of the room, a hatch opened, depositing the living bodies of children where hooded practitioners cut their bodies open to extract their livers.

I once described this dream to a colleague, wondering whether, at the same time reflecting my own trauma, it might not have referred to the human experiments actually being conducted at that time in Nazi concentration camps, although those horrifying truths had yet to be revealed. He affirmed his belief that often children "see" things far removed in space and time and person. If, later on in adulthood, they remember them at all, they realize that such phenomena seemed at the time in no way out of the ordinary, although often the surrounding adults had been too preoccupied—or too frightened—to notice.

Occasionally we find these phenomena still present in adults. I remember when, at the age of 18, I finally put together all the mysterious puzzle pieces of my father's life—stories he and others had told me, including the first articulation of the meaning of homosexuality—to grasp what my father had been concealing from me all my life. I shared my dawning awareness with a classmate. The very next day, I heard my father remark: "I know what you have been telling your friends about me behind my back." To this day I believe that is exactly what I heard, and not what I imagined.

Poets are often identified as prophets, and perhaps they draw on such mysterious capacities as children do. I remember being quite startled when Tillie Olson once observed that the Book of Revelations must surely be the greatest poem ever written. I remember in particular a night long years ago when unable to sleep, I came to the notion that I must be wanting to avoid dreaming a dream waiting to be admitted from the antechamber of my mind. I rose from bed to sit at my keyboard. A story emerged. It concluded with the arrival of mysterious stagehands who raised the entire dream landscape into the flies as if it were stage scenery. It marked the point where I traded my life in the theater for the writing of fiction. But in the actual writing I clearly visualized the distant Manhattan skyline, its tallest buildings consumed by flames.

Although I am hardly an authority on the shamanic trance states of people living in tribal cultures the world over, I trust implicitly the account of my colleague, public artist Lauren Elder, who in a co-authored book, *And I Alone Survived,* tells the story of her rescue following a plane crash in the High Sierra. Lauren is a person of strongly Western sensibilities, whose feet are firmly planted on very down-to-earth ground. During the 16-hour period she walked out from the high summit of the Sierra, although seriously wounded and in shock, she was able to scale down a 100-foot rock face, and walk through the Owens Valley desert to reach the nearest town. During her ordeal, she claims to have seen people she would actually meet two weeks later in the course of her recovery. When at last she reached civilization, horrified onlookers pointed out the deep gash in her arm. She had not exsanguinated in all that time, evidently because the severity of her injury had induced in her a state of shock.

Reading "Lily Mind," readers will have many recollections of their own. These are not so much intimations of immortality as they are traces of the immortality of these many gifts that humans, especially children and poets, may still share with animals in minds uncluttered by the distractions and detritus of so-called "civilization." Call it our original self, which our upbringing, and our learning lives have de-educated out of us, sometimes subtly, sometimes with a razor strop, as the great filmmaker, Ingmar Bergman suffered at his minister-father's hands for being what his father called a "liar." Perhaps it is what millennia later, churchmen like to call "Original Sin." But these ancient gifts may have been a way of guarding us against all of present civilization's pitfalls: unawareness, indifference, blindness, and selfishness. Perhaps they were the illuminations, which once reminded us of the connectedness of all things. Without their avail, we grope the dark night without a guide. Our epilogue as a civilization reflects how we built and conquered empires, a dreary and short chapter, and the forlorn conclusion of a predictable story. What great turn in the road might we have missed?

III.

TWISTS IN THE ROAD

23. Disappearance of the Great Axicon

In all of your deliberations in the Confederate Council, in your efforts at law making, in all your official acts, self-interest shall be cast into oblivion.... Look and listen for the welfare of the whole people and have always in view not only the present but also the coming generations, even those whose faces are yet beneath the surface of the ground—the unborn of the future Nation.

—Constitution of the Iroquois Nation

Exactly 100 years after James Watt patented the first coal-fired steam engine, Augustin Mouchot published his manifesto, *Chaleur Solaire: Applications Industrielles*. "One must not believe, despite the silence of modern writings, that the idea of using solar heat for mechanical operations is recent. On the contrary..., this idea is very ancient and its slow development across the centuries has given birth to various curious devices." One of those so-called curious devices was Mouchot's own invention, an axicon, or solar dish, capable of focusing the sun's heat, in appearance much like a dish antenna, whose prototype he first displayed in 1869. But by then, the price of coal had dropped so significantly that if people took note at all of his invention, it appeared laughingly irrelevant because when push comes to shove, money trumps all other considerations. Nonetheless Mouchot persisted.

Watt's skies were clear in 1736, the year of his birth, but by the time Mouchot made his appearance in 1825, the skies had already begun to cloud as we can see depicted in Philippe de Loutherbourg's 1801 painting "Coalbrookdale by Night." And indeed, if we look at the many representations Camille Pissarro made of the great Bridge at Rouen, his brushwork attests to the choking pollution spewing from the factories located on the far bank of the Loire.

But unlike Watt, who was born into the merchant class with little awareness other than his penchant for mechanics and mathematics, Mouchot was a man of culture and learning. In his manifesto quoted above, he traced the focusing of solar light from its discovery in Ancient Egypt, through Greece, and to its application by the Arabs to produce heat. But aside from the year in which the French Ministry of Education gave him a grant and leave of absence to perfect his invention in Algeria, his first commitment was to teaching. He seems not to have had Watt's awareness that to develop his invention for practical applications he would need a moneyed partner. Also unlike Watt, his thought was able to project the future. "Eventually industry will no longer find in Europe the resources to satisfy its prodigious expansion.... Coal will undoubtedly be used up. What will industry do then?"

Mouchot made those observations in 1878, the year he exhibited at the *Exposition Universelle* in Paris the great axicon he had perfected in Algeria. His earlier model, the prototype of 1869, was to disappear in the chaos and destruction of the Franco-Prussian War, a war in which, with the German annexation of the mining district of Alsace-Lorraine, France lost its access to cheap coal—which may partly explain why present-day France is the European country most relying on nuclear energy, despite the catastrophic risks it represents as we are now learning from the runaway planetary disaster still unfolding in Japan.

Because Western consciousness seems largely unable or unwilling to consider consequences—unlike the awareness of the much more enlightened Iroquois who considered a future "unto seven generations"—it did not foresee the growing competition by nations for resources, although with the Franco-Prussian war of 1870-71, the trend of wars for resources had already become evident. It could not or would not foresee the global convulsions of the oil, and more recently the natural gas wars of the 21st Century centered in the Middle East, and expanding to Libya and most recently to the Ukraine and Syria, nor the resulting displacement and death by sanction and starvation and the use of "depleted" uranium in a nuclear war against millions of people of the Middle East—the very people who first experimented with focusing the sun's light to produce heat. It could not or would not foresee the consequences of drilling through shale to produce natural gas, contaminating whole aquifers, and depriving growing numbers of people of pure drinking and irrigation water. It could not foresee the vandalism of destroying whole mountains to grab easy fossil fuel pickings, or of dumping the resulting sludge into mountain streams and communities, choking the air and contaminating the water; it could not foresee the ultimate insanity of designing nuclear plants and marketing them throughout the world—as GE did—knowing they had a 90 percent probability of containment failure. It could not foresee, or even momentarily consider what that "failure" might actually mean for a planet over which the sword of terminal nuclear contamination now hangs by a technological thread. It could not foresee that science for all its cleverness would far exceed its ability to control the genie it had pushed out of the jar to a most abortive birth.

Call it Disappearance of a Great Axiom that goes: Never buy anything you can never hope to pay for. But in the West, and particularly in the United States of Credit, it's full speed ahead. In the industrial world's profit casino, who pays attention to such antiquated notions nowadays?

24. The Long and Arduous Journey

Transformative change has moved from the slow arithmetic progression of prehistory, into an ever-accelerating modern age. Primates have been playing with stones for nearly three million years with very little advancement. Two and a half million years ago, as the hominid line began its differentiation away from its apelike ancestor, *Homo habilis* took the apes' simple rock, capable of smashing, and began refining its shape, chipping away to create a sharper edge. But *Homo habilis'* small, one-pint-sized brain kept him using this tool for very nearly the next million years until two-pint brained *Homo erectus* discovered that by chipping away at *both* sides of the stone, he could fashion the more effective bifacial hand axe, a tool which has been found wherever he migrated, in Africa,

Asia and Europe, with essentially no technological improvement for the next roughly 800,000 years.

Some one hundred and fifty thousand years ago, *Homo sapiens sapiens* emerged, now with a three-pint brain, but very little change seems to be evident until—suddenly—and almost wherever they roamed—there's evidence of a phase change, one characterized by a great eruption of art, of burial practices, and creation of a rich variety of artifacts.

But the great turning point hastening the separation between humankind and our awareness of the natural world must be situated at the start of the Industrial Revolution whose eddies are now being felt throughout the world. Not that the movement towards urbanization begun in the Renaissance and the mechanistic view of the Enlightenment did not lay in the groundwork. Yet the size of typical urban populations at the time of the Renaissance had not made the geometric leap brought about by the economic pressures at the time of the Industrial Revolution, which drew people who had inhabited the countryside, subsistence farmers and cottage craftsmen, to flock to urban centers to work in factories, and in the coalmines.

Like it or not, landscape imprints all people. Although my own origins are in the concrete world of New York City where often rogue sumac trees pierce broken sidewalks, and manicured street trees confined to iron cages are the only green to be found anywhere, of all the landscapes of California, I most favor the desert with its vast expanses of apparent emptiness. On those rare occasions when I share my preference, more often than not, people are aghast. Over time I have come to realize it's because they fear the desert. They fear it because the sound of the air passing through sage is very different from sounds more familiar to them, but of which they are not consciously aware, of wind riffling the leaves of deciduous trees.

Laurens van der Post writes about the Kalahari:

> ...I found new freedom for my senses in the [desert,] so concrete...that it was as if a great physical burden had been lifted from me.... What a growing relief it was not to be solicited

by the noise...of my own metropolitan time.... That freedom had a voice of its own, too, for we all spoke instinctively in tones that we did not normally use and which came from us as naturally as the sound of wind from the trees.

How often do we consider *sound*-as-landscape? The sense of hearing seems to resonate with the snake brain, where the most basic tropisms seem to be located. It is the last sense to depart the dying body. Imagine now the sounds attendant on life lived in the factories of the late 18th century, the sounds accompanying working sixteen hours a day in the mines. The clanking, the screeching, the smashing, the hammering, the drilling, the crashing of great iron weights, the roar of the blast furnaces, the throb and pound of machinery. Sixteen hours a day, seven days a week. How long might it take to wipe out all memory of wind in the grass, of birdsong, of rainfall on the earth?

And later, with the coming of gaslight and shortly thereafter, the incandescent bulb, how long would it take to forget the hallucinatory color of the gloaming? How long to forget moonlight turning countryside to silver or the wheel of the night sky? How long to forget the rising of the moon or the rosy light of morning? Yet all these things remind us of the beauty of where we live. Remind us that we inhabit a rotating ball that turns day into night, and night again into day. Winter into spring, and spring into fall. Drought into flood, and flood into drought. How long to exchange time measured by the very slow spread of light on the landscape, for the speed up of factory, or mine, or of boardrooms where money is time, and time, money, and where workers become cogs in the machinery of profit, to be hired at the lowest wages?

The harnessing of electricity, and more recently human reliance on such technologies as industrial chemistry, Wi-Fi, television and computers, and the growth of social media—to say nothing of socio-political changes—have produced the profound kinds of brain changes that may very well have crowded out or somehow occluded our much earlier, extra-sensorial ways of inhabiting our planet. (Ironically, a 2013 UCLA symposium advanced a newly developing scientific technology where a wired human brain in one location could directly control the physical behavior of another distant individual whose brain had been similarly wired.)

Yet these turnings—mechanization of production, the age of electricity, "free" markets—are considered progress by most without the backward glance that asks, what have they made of us? What have we lost? What have they done to our sense of being-in-the-world? What kind of new man and new woman have they wrought? And how far and how long have the new man and new woman had to travel to come to the point now of planetary destruction brought about by automobile exhaust, oil drilling, coal firing, fracking, strip mining, mountaintop removal, dumping in the seas, waterways and soils of barrels of chemical contaminants and nuclear waste; how long to suffer disease and death from nuclear technology, and the nuclear war spreading U_{238} since 1999 over Kosovo, Iraq, Afghanistan, Yemen, and Somalia, and most recently, Fukushima's now 4 quadrillion Becquerels of contaminated water pouring daily into the sea? Lulled in the sleep of privilege, we remember the sound of wind only in our dreams.

We walk the alien streets of cities boxed in a concrete cell, forgetful of the earth which gave us life, or if not us, those in distant generations who may still have felt attachment to the soil. Many of the eighty men and a few women of the world whose wealth equals that of the bottom half of the world's population (3,500,000,000 people) some of whom make decisions at the Bilderberg Meetings for the entire human race are—some of them—descended from an aristocracy which lost contact with the soil as far back as the eighteenth century, a few even earlier; the remainder *arrivistes*, landlords and financiers whose immense wealth allowed them to cut the umbilical cord to the Earth's womb, some of them even earlier than the nineteenth century. Most of them have never held a clod of earth in their hands except possibly to break ground for an industrial installation. (And the meaning: to break the *tradition* of ground—not just its physical aspect.)

Consider this admission by David Rockefeller at the Bilderberg Meetings of 1991: "We are grateful to the *Washington Post, The New York Times, Time Magazine* and other great publications whose directors have attended our meetings and respected their promises of discretion for almost 40 years. It would have been impossible for us to develop our plan for the world if we had been subjected to the lights of publicity during those years. But the world is more sophisticated and prepared to march towards a world government. The supranational sovereignty of an intellectual elite and world bankers is surely preferable to the national auto-determination practiced in past centuries." The invitees to these meetings, are, almost all of them millionaires if not billionaires, among them royalty, bankers, directors of corporations, media giants, university heads, prime ministers, and American politicians—Rockefeller and Kissinger among its longest attendees.

Consider, too, how custom and prejudice have worked to exile whole peoples from the natural world. For that matter, notice how few in our cities pay attention to anything but the i-Phones glued fast as bionic appendages to their ears. Read there *escape,* something that has become a virtual meme, escape from the dehumanization of urbanized life, a life that human beings were never meant to inhabit, regardless of our apparent and unconscious adaptations. Yet in the evolution of a race, which calls itself human, all our "civilizing" changes, every one, occupy not even one percent of the timespan of our existence.

24. Axle and Wheel

I am trying to understand being born to the urge to destroy, to rip mountains apart, to pour thousand-year poison into the seas, to belch soot into the sky, to kill everything that lives. Where does it start, this impulse? In what mind? What axel drives this wheel?

—Cecile Pineda, *Devil's Tango*

Although it's good to start out with a question, not all questions start out good. In *Apology to a Whale* I have framed my original inquiry in the light of other intelligences, namely that of beings other than human that share the planet with *homo sapiens sapiens.* I began to think about speech and the use of language as a possible factor: what did primates lose when they acquired the power of speech and the use of language? Somehow I intuited that somewhere, wrapped up in the issue of human language, an answer might present itself, but I came to understand that my question needed further refinement. I began to consider *what connection might exist between language and the suicidal behavior of mankind? And which mankind? And why?*

In the absence of writing, the narrative of pre-literate civilizations is recorded in the burial offerings found in their grave sites. Through her lifetime of work documenting such sites, Marija Gimbutas was able to describe the dynamic civilization that existed 3,500 years, from 7,000 through 3,500 B.C. She called it the Civilization of Old Europe. It occupied the area from what we now call Austria and Czechoslovakia to areas bordering the Black Sea, including the Balkans, a part of present-day Southern Italy, Turkey, Greece, Crete, and the Ukraine, a vast area roughly spanning modern-day Vienna to Kiev.

Prior to Gimbutas' study, little substantive information had been paid to civilizations like that of Old Europe that worshiped the Great Goddess. Gimbutas changed all that, much to the distress, and sometime outrage of her male colleagues, and even of feminists who were all too happy to dismiss her work on grounds of sentimentality! By the time I heard her talk in Berkeley just before she died, she had published her great works, *The Civilization of the Goddess* and *The Language of the Goddess.* Her many books are filled with careful documentation of thousands of artifacts excavated at hundreds of tells located throughout a vast region of Eurasia. Her photographs and drawings show ceramics and sculptures, and both household and sacred vessels and utensils, as well as costumes, masks, palm-sized figurines of the Great Goddess, depictions of female goddesses and male gods, and miniature temples and shrines. She demonstrated how, object by object, these burial offerings carry the symbolic narrative of this pre-literate civilization.

She offered evidence that the number and style of female graves matched those of males, indicating that wealth was distributed equally and pointing to the civilization's non-hierarchical social organization. It was a matrilineal society, reflecting its worship of the Great Goddess; it did not ascribe dominance to one gender over another. Women and homosexuals were held in as high regard as men. Agriculture was developed by women. People hunted, and gathered; they supplemented their diet cultivating barley, wheat, vetch, peas and other legumes. They traded over vast distances for obsidian, alabaster, marble and spondylus shell, and this trade provided the kind of cross fertilization vital to cultural growth.

In all, Gimbutas identified seven subgroupings, not all of them spanning the full 3,500-year range of time. Although she describes two of these subgroupings as having been surrounded by fortifications and watchtowers, nowhere is there evidence of warfare or contest for territory. In no Old Europe burial sites were weapons ever found, indicating that the society was a peaceful one. Yet all were disrupted by the invasion during the fifth millennium B.C. by the Kurgans, ancestors of semi-nomadic Indo-Europeans, (named after the Russian word for their burial sites). Theirs was a grab for new grazing territory that lasted 1,500 years, driving the worshippers of the Great Goddess as far west as the British Isles, France, Spain, into the Basque country, and possibly even as far west as what is now Vermont.

Had the Kurgan Proto-Indo-European speakers been pacific agriculturists as Colin Renfrew and a few other archeologists contend, we might expect their language to have offered root words for grains and cereals. Instead, the presence of weapons in their burial sites gives evidence of a war-like people, given to conquest and violence, whereas although the graves of the earlier people show no such evidence, their skeletons often show marks of violence, such as skulls bashed in from behind, probably because the people of the older civilization were being put to flight.

Besides weapons and warfare, the Kurgans brought with them a hierarchical social organization as reflected in the vast disparities in their burial sites; a religion which worshipped a male sky god; *but above all, the language they spoke, identified by linguists as Proto-Indo-European, a paradigm shift which would determine the future history of the West to the present day.* Notwithstanding, Gimbutas is careful to make the point that although the ideology of Proto-Indo-Europeans succeeded that of the Old Europeans, the process was somewhat syncretic, meaning that to this day, vestiges of the older ways are still to be found in Europe, particularly on the littoral, in such isolated pockets as Brittany, and the Basque Country.

The origins of Proto-Indo-European (PIE) are to be found in Sanskrit which shares cognates (that is, similar-sounding words) with all Kurgan-derived European languages that developed to the west of what is modern-day India: Balto-Slavic, Greek, Armenian, Germanic, Italic, Celtic, and Tocharian (a now extinct language

Proto-Indo-European Language Groups

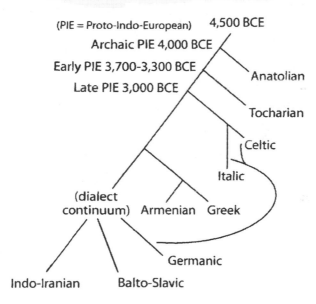

Figure 2. Branching diagram (according to Ringe/Warnow/Taylor) showing minimal separation dates, as PIE split off into Europe's proto-language groups. (Germanic is shown late because it also shared many Pre-Baltic and Pre-Slavic traits.)

spoken at one time in what is now China). Only four European languages—Finnish, Hungarian, Basque, and Estonian—are non-Proto-Indo-European-derived. All the modern-day Proto-Indo-European-derived languages possess nouns, pronouns, or other parts of speech *marking for gender* except for the first language to branch off, Proto-Anatolian. Although not a PIE-derived language, modern Turkish shares this same characteristic.

Few traces exist of the pre-Kurgan language of Old Europe. In the early 1900s, amongst Knossos' Bronze Age ruins, and at the Minoan Palace at Haghia Triada, Sir Arthur Evans unearthed a number of stones bearing two writing systems, the Greek of Linear B, dating from about 1450 B.C. which was deciphered by Michael Ventris before his untimely death in 1956, and the other, Linear A, which has yet to be deciphered. Although similar in alphabet, Linear A records an unknown language.*

According to Marija Gimbutas,** traces of its use have been found as early as 5,300 to 4,300 B.C. However, all evidence of the spoken language itself seems to have been lost, perhaps permanently.

Also according to Gimbutas,*** unlike the people of the Old Europe civilization, the Kurgan Proto-Indo-Europeans, as herdsmen—and characteristically of nomadic peoples—built no temples. But the iconic figuration on their anthropomorphic stelae (upright stone slabs set in the ground like gravestones) reveals their hierarchical ideology. Incised as warrior bodies wearing the

---

* We might look to one of the four European languages not derived from PIE for the derivate of the language spoken by the people of the Civilization of Old Europe; and if we consider westward population displacement patterns following the Kurgan-led PIE conquest, the likely place to look is the littoral, the place where further escape is no longer possible except by sea. Predictably, Basque seems to be the candidate. This speculation is confirmed by Gimbutas in her 1991-published work, *The Civilization of the Goddess*. With this piece of the puzzle, it may be possible to finally decode Linear A, which might tell us something we need to know.
** Gimbutas: *Civilization of The Goddess,* pp 352, 354
*** Gimbutas: *Civilization of the Goddess*, pp. 398-9

emblem of their sky god, worn as a solar disk neck ornament, they are adorned with daggers, shafted halberds, axes, bows, arrows, quivers, and with horses and other grazing animals, some of them draft oxen yoked to wheeled wagons.

Whereas the main theme of the religion of Old Europe—evoking the sacred round of birth, life, death, and rebirth—was the parthenogenetic Goddess as the source of life, the Kurgan Proto-Indo-European pantheon instead denotes, to quote Gimbutas, *"a socially and economically* oriented ideology" (itals. added) consisting of male gods who rode horses, wielded weapons and who were associated both with life-creating and death-wielding attributes—*but not rebirth.*

Any Kurgan female goddesses functioned merely as brides or consorts of male gods. Fallen heroes were glorified sometimes to the point of deification. In contrast to Old European ideology as reflected in their communal burials, the Kurgan Proto-Europeans saw a direct, linear continuity of the *individual* from the physical world into the afterlife, for which they required personal *property.*

Gimbutas concludes:

> The collapse of Old Europe coincides with the process of Indo-Europeanization of Europe…leading to a drastic cultural change reminiscent of the conquest of the American continent. Archeological evidence, supported by comparative Indo-European linguistics and mythology, suggests a clash of two ideologies, social structures, and economics perpetrated by trauma-inducing institutions.…
>
> [Their] tombs…were reserved for the warrior elite [who were buried with] their favorite war gear, the spear, bow and arrow, and flint dagger or long knife.
>
> The gentle agriculturalists…were easy prey to the war-like Kurgan horsemen.… From the middle of the 5th millennium B.C., the swift horse became a carrier of unrest that continued for millennia. If we look back at European history, at the routine massacres by horse-riding people—even the Christian Crusaders—we see how violence, abetted by the rise of the swift horse, became a dominant aspect of life.*

---

* Gimbutas: *Civilization of The Goddess,* pp 352, 354

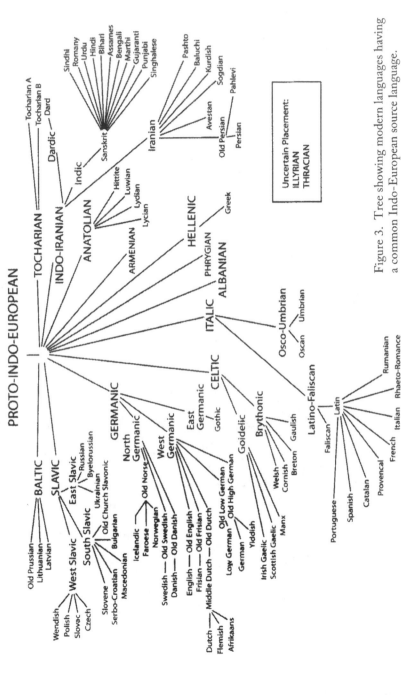

PROTO-INDO-EUROPEAN

Uncertain Placement:
ILLYRIAN
THRACIAN

Figure 3. Tree showing modern languages having a common Indo-European source language.

In *The Horse, the Wheel and Language,* David W. Anthony substantiates Gimbutas' findings. He describes the Kurgan Proto-Indo-European (PIE) civilization, illustrating his work with linguistic charts. His images of artifacts recovered from PIE burial ground excavations consistently bear evidence of a hierarchically organized society: no women are ever buried separately; chiefs and other prominent figures are buried in full regalia, with their weapons and a wealth of personal ornaments. In those excavations found in the central European plane, in what is now Germany, and I might point out, more recently the area where Nazism originated, Kurgan graves show evidence of *suttee*, that is, sacrifice of wives, children, and attendants, who were seen as chattel.

Aside from archeological evidence, much is revealed about the social organization of pre-historical cultures by a study of language and etymology. The Kurgan Proto-Indo-European evidence is no exception. As cited by Gimbutas,* the Kurgan PIE words for sister is *swes:r,* which means "to own;" the word for widow, *wydh* means "to be empty or inadequate," but there is no corresponding similarity of the words for a bride's family. The word *wedh* for "bride price" derives from the word meaning "to lead," suggesting chattel. But the word *pot* denotes the male family head or chief, prompting Gimbutas to conclude, "The picture of an Indo-European community leader painted by mythological and legal texts appears to be a despotic, and probably polygynous, warrior patriarch who ruled his family and clan with absolute power over life and death."

What is the connection between European languages that derive from Kurgan Proto-Indo-European and the history of Western civilization? Is it possible that if we speak a Proto-Indo-European-derived language, English in particular, our language might reflect the legacy of a distant but related culture that denigrated women, that advanced a male sky-god, suppressing worship of the Great Goddess. That embraced warfare and organized itself along non-egalitarian lines? How would that language imprint

---

* Gimbutas: *Civilization of the Goddess,* p. 395

us? Would our culture privilege all things legendarily associated with the male: hunting, killing, aggression, victory, conquest, brute strength, power, hierarchy, militarism, weaponry, acquisition, and control? Would it devalue nature, altruism, tenderness, nurture, compassion, conflict resolution, and child bearing? Would it privilege power relations favoring men, especially men of a dominant race and class? What evidence would its myths and legends point to in terms of its dominant paradigm?

According to linguist Christopher Ehret, the Proto-Indo-European root language gave rise to literatures rife with accounts of fighting and warfare. "We find preserved in early myths and legends almost everywhere among Indo-Europeans a glorification of battle, and particularly of death in battle, not entirely unknown elsewhere in the world, but of an intensity not often matched. We also find...in these stories a division of society that singles out warriors as an elite group..." reflected in such myths of the hero as the Norse sagas, *Beowulf*, the Legends of Cuchulain, Roland, El Cid, and Tirant lo Blanc.

According to Peter Wells, writing about the Bronze and Iron ages, in *How Ancient Europeans Saw the World: Visions, Patterns, and the Shaping of the Mind in Prehistoric Times*, even as late as 2,000 to 200 B.C., burial sites excavated in Bohemia, Germany, France, and as far west as Britain still contained not only weapons, but parts of wagons such as axels and wheels, and often—unlike later royal and "ship" burials—these artifacts are found to be ritually broken, bent, or otherwise defaced.

IV.

LANGUAGE AS MIRROR

26. The Voice that Commands

The values a society lives by [determine] not only its socio-technical structure but also its world view, knowledge, scientific enterprise, and economic system. Values are integrally related with epistemology, and since both individuals and societies are faced with the...dilemma that there is always an infinite number of phenomena and sets of data to examine, the choice of what realities to pay attention to is always value-based. Once cultures...have codified [them,] these values...represent the parameters of their...choices..., social adaptation, regeneration, and cultural evolution.

—Hazel Henderson: *The Politics of the Solar Age*

In most of the linguistic literature, Proto-Indo-European (PIE) is referred to as the mother tongue, the root of almost all European languages spoken by the Western world, and all the PIE-derived languages are identified as daughter languages. One of many striking ironies is why the language of a patriarchal, warlike, male-sky-god-worshipping Proto-Indo-European people who replaced the pacific Goddess-worshipping culture of Old Europe should be called anything but a Father tongue, and its derivates anything but son languages.

English and its ultimate source language, Proto-Indo-European, both lay out a particular worldview. At this historical moment, the power dynamics of world domination and the language of world commerce still find themselves in the hands of English language speakers, primarily those born and those educated in the United States. The World Bank and IMF, representing the Western nations and their financial interests, are the greatest purveyors of poverty throughout the world despite their rhetorical claims to the contrary. The U.S. and its NATO surrogates have become the bully-policemen of the world. Of the twenty-eight NATO member nations, only three do not speak a language derived from Proto-Indo-European. On the diplomatic-control front, of the United Nation's five permanent Security Council members, four are speakers of Proto-Indo-European-derived languages. The only exception is China. Of the ten non-permanent members, four are countries speaking proto-Indo-European-derived languages. To sum up: non-Proto-Indo-European-derived languages are represented in only one out of five among the permanent members, those holding veto rights; and in six out of ten among the non-permanent members.

Language is the lens through which we apprehend the world. It circumscribes our perception of it, including our cosmology and our worldview, and determines how we live and interact with each other and with the planet. It is the voice that commands. Forms of speech reflect—sometimes cryptically—the deep assumptions of a culture and, in turn, perpetuate them.

Although not a trained linguist himself, Benjamin Whorf's contribution to the field of relative linguistics is still a benchmark, even though his works were published—many of them—after his death in 1941 at 44 years of age. His comparative studies in relative linguistics focused on a number of Native American languages, chief among them Hopi. An example might be Whorf's discussion of the Hopi, who speak of clouds in their prayers for rain as if clouds were alive. The Hopi word for clouds, ʔo.'maw, is "always pluralized in the animate way." Therefore grammarians know that clouds belong to what Whorf called the "*cryptotype* of animatedness," something that is hidden to the observer at first blush, but *deeply* embedded in the Hopi language as such. In any number of instances, the Hopi discriminates between subtle distinctions with utter simplicity* "for the forms of speech have accustomed him to do so.... English compared to Hopi is like a *bludgeon* compared to a rapier" [italics added].

---

* For example, in Hopi there is no time as we construe it: no past, present or future. Existence is marked by what is manifest, and what is manifesting.

Whorf sums up the notion that language, worldview, and human behavior itself are inextricably linked:

> …Every language is a vast pattern-system, different from others, in which are culturally obtained the forms and categories by which the personality not only communicates, but also analyzes nature, notices or neglects types of relationship and phenomena, channels his reason, and builds the house of his consciousness.

Now let us imagine that we occupy the interior of a hollow ball of yarn, barely able to peer through its latticework. Beyond the barrier, we imagine there must be freedom to apprehend the world objectively, that is, without cultural constraints of any kind, whether imposed by upbringing or language. But when we peer through the narrow slits between the fibers, we realize that our ball of yarn inhabits another hollow ball of yarn, and to our dismay, we realize that in turn that ball of yarn occupies the interior of yet another ball of yarn. This is the constraint imposed by our cultural bonds mediated among others, through the Proto-Indo-European-derived language we happen to speak. It pulls the proverbial wool over our eyes. It is a language which inevitably has shaped, circumscribed, and perpetuated our world view, ordered our existence, governed our interactions, and imprinted our identity from the time we were born—and long before—because it has been handed down, like some epistemological DNA, from deep within the past of our hierarchical and war-like ancestry.

Now imagine for a moment that we were born into a small, beleaguered tribe of Northern Californian Indians, the Wintu; that Wintu was our mother tongue and that we knew no other. Our sense of our own bodies would tell us we belonged to the Earth because we could only distinguish our right from our left hand or other body part in relation to its relative proximity to a specific feature of our landscape, a river perhaps, or a hill. Depending on which way we faced we would identify our ear ache as hurting, say, not as our left ear, but riverside or to the south. But because we could never possess the Earth, we would be unable to say that a certain river ran to our left or right. We would have to describe it as running to the west, or the south, or east, or north. Would we own the landscape? Or would we live in it as a part of it?

If we spoke Wintu, we would never be able to allude to possession of another living thing. Not even a baby. We would have to refer to it as the baby or child "who lives with us." I admit to cringing whenever I hear a man referring to "my wife," but if we spoke Wintu, if we wanted to allude to a spouse, we would have to say, "I am husbanded by...," or "I am wived by...." How would that affect our sense of possession? And our sense of power relations? If we spoke Wintu, we would have no relative pronoun marker for gender, only a gender-neutral word that could refer either to a man or woman. Would we be inclined to see the women—and the men—in our world in terms of a different dominance relationship? We could not describe a relative or friend as sick. We would have to say, "I am sick with respect to my mother, or with respect to my friend." Would we be inclined more keenly to feel someone else's pain?

Supposing we couldn't spotlight an individual of any category, whether person or animal. Instead, to pinpoint an individual we would have to add a small suffix meaning "that" ("that" bear, "that" tree). Would we be more inclined to see the whole of the world in each of its parts? Would we be inclined to hold all living beings in respect, and accord animals and persons each their separate dignity?

Suppose we needed to describe some event. If we spoke Wintu, we would have to let our narrative carry information specifying whether we actually saw it with our own eyes, or whether it had been told to us, or whether we inferred it but didn't actually see it. There could be no Wintu edition of the *New York Times*.

It is said that among speakers of Nahuatl, the indigenous language of much of Mexico, spoken by people who still keep to the Old Way, elaborate rituals of greeting are the habit, precluding any urge to "get to the point" so favored by hurried Western ways of discourse. By contrast, here, in every-day America, we greet other people or even address them in writing with "Hey!" And prisoners at Guantanamo, most of them not guilty of any war crimes, there only because someone sold them for bounty, are referred to as "packages."

From Wintu and other non-Indo-European examples, we can extrapolate how much language circumscribes worldview with respect to either a collaborative (we) or hierarchical (I) view of the world, affecting attitudes towards gender, sense of possession and power relations. Although presumably "civilized," we might discover how really limited we are in contrast to people the White European world has been quite satisfied to dismiss historically as savages.

Before contact in 1770, the Wintu had settled in the Sacramento, McCloud and Trinity River watersheds, and may have numbered in the thousands, but their numbers were decimated by malaria and massacres—notably led by such frontier pioneers as Fremont and Kit Carson—and poisonings by neighborly white settlers eager to invite them to a "friendship" feast. A 1990 U.S. Census lists Wintu as having only six remaining speakers.*

Some years ago, my colleague Maria Gilardin, founder of TUC Radio, shared with me her behind-the-scenes experience recording a historic event for TUC. After many years of appealing to the UN for redress against the theft of their land by Peabody Coal, and their forced relocation, at last the United Nations agreed to send a representative to the Big Mountain Diné (Navajo) to take their testimony. Gilardin's recording of the Diné elders speaking on behalf of their entire tribe presents a challenge to Western ears. The elders are not in a hurry. They are very old people, their voices

---

* A study by Hallet, et al., looked at a number of cultural variables and found that language loss had the highest correlation with First Nations youth suicide. In a study including 150 tribes in British Columbia, they found that, where fewer than half the elders still knew their original language, the young were six times more likely to commit suicide. Depriving a people of their language deprives them of their history and with it their identity. It also deprives those who study linguistics of valuable templates which reveal the hidden assumptions underlying their own languages.

are cracked, the words hesitating, the language of exchange is not their own. They are speaking at the level of discourse we identify as poetry. And like much indigenous poetry, it becomes the repetitive poetry of song.

Midway through their testimony, the UN representative excused himself. Had he become impatient? Did he expect them to get right to the point? or perhaps plead with him? Or beg? Did he find their words tedious, lacking in focus, or devoid of concrete proposals? Would it have been more to their advantage had they spoken in their native dialect of Navajo, with simultaneous translation? Did their use of English in respectful deference to the UN representative place them at a disadvantage? And what meaning might he have taken from their calling for respect for Mother Earth?

After the UN representative walked out, both Maria Gilardin, and the attending videographer continued taping. That day they were the only representatives of the White European World willing to pay appropriate respect and to stay long enough to hear the Diné out.

The Navajo (Diné) Resettlement Act of 1974 reflects the genocidal posture towards Native Americans that the U.S. has always maintained, either through the "law," or through military violence. To illustrate: with the support of Senators Kerry and Kennedy of Massachusetts and Senator Rockefeller of West Virginia, U.S. war "hero" Senator John McCain was able to intervene personally on behalf of Peabody Coal to pass the act by forging Diné signatures on the resettlement agreement, thus enabling the theft of Diné land, granted them by treaty, and forcing their relocation to Church Rock, a New Mexico site so contaminated with uranium tailings it has the highest rate of birth defects in the U.S., and some 7,000 have died there since 1999.

In early hemispheric history, following contact, Native Americans sometimes referred to Europeans as "the people who beat their children." As a child, McCain was so severely beaten by his parents that he protected himself by losing consciousness. His parents warned him that, should he force himself to lose consciousness again, they would retaliate. Their remedy was to throw him unconscious into a bathtub of ice water. Evidently they were preparing him to assume his world-famous role of war hero and torture survivor at the hands of the North Vietnamese. As a musician he acquired a national reputation for his 2007 vocals: "Bomb, Bomb, Bomb Iran."*

27. Women Before And After Monotheism

In light of the pass humanity has come to, living as it does on a planet where perpetual wars are now the rule, and where conflict engenders spreading conflict as we see at present in Africa and the Middle East, and now Eurasia; where technology has gone beyond the limits of its own expertise, as we saw with the BP (British Petroleum) Gulf "spill" (more appropriately called a hemorrhage) of 2010, and the still-looming Fukushima planetary catastrophe originating in 2011, it may help to take the measure of how deeply entrenched are our gender and power relations.

In the era before Herodotus—probably the first to write what we think of as history—human affairs were couched in metaphor. The twice-told story of Adam and Eve raises not only gender but religious issues as well in that part of the parable where Eve partakes of the Tree of Knowledge at the urging of a serpent. The serpent is one of the many representations of the Great Goddess. The myth refers to a time when there was among the Ancient Israelites, a kind of backsliding where they reverted—some of them— to worship of the Goddess. Clearly, among patriarchal people that sort of thing had to stop. An avenging angel brandishing a fiery sword—a stand-in male emblem—swiftly expelled both Adam and Eve from the Garden—a stand-in female emblem—reminding the faithful that there was no room for syncretism in a religion that enshrined an exclusive, vengeful, jealous, and war-like male sky-god.

---

*See http://www.informationclearinghouse.info/article37338.htm.

Many of the same historical events first couched in myth, legend, and epic came to be reflected later in the Greek drama. In 1976, a fellow director suggested that our company produce *Medea*, Euripides' tragedy first performed in 431 B.C. In the original play, Medea, a royal woman from the kingdom of Colchis, is tricked by Jason who abducts her to his kingdom of Corinth where he marries and eventually abandons her. She takes revenge by killing her own two small sons sired by him and by murdering his new wife, Glauce. The chorus expresses horror, but also sympathy because Medea vicariously rights the wrongs suffered by all abandoned women.

The patriarchal aspects of Euripides' drama have always struck me as sensational—and questionable—probably why *Medea* has appealed to generation after generation of theater-goers with surprisingly little objection by feminists of the present day. But what was the layer that came before history was re-written by a patriarchy which has held sway over Western human affairs ever since the emergence—and control by men—of literacy and probably way before? I looked to Robert Graves for the earlier variants of Euripides' *Medea*.

According to Graves, because the Corinthians did not want to be depicted in an unfavorable light, they "bribed Euripides with fifteen talents of silver to absolve them from guilt, pretending that Medea killed two of her own children, and that the remainder perished in the palace to which she had set fire." But the pre-classic myth has the Corinthians stoning Medea's many children to death. This, and her later wanderings—to Thebes, to Athens, to Thessaly, and finally back to Colchis—may suggest that, with the ascent of the patriarchy, the shrines of the Great Goddess had to be abandoned one by one throughout Asia Minor. We decided to offer our own version of *Medea* instead.

Leonard Shlain in *Sex, Time and Power* proposes the idea that when human beings began to connect menstruation with the phases of the moon, they were able to begin to think about deep time and to confront mortality, and that when they connected intercourse with birth, men began to exercise control over woman's reproduction, which still seems to be the case to this day. In the present world, deeply embedded as we are in the cultural assumptions of patriarchy, it is extremely difficult to separate out from all the mores we take for granted exactly how even the most subtle societal gender-controls color human behavior. So mired in habit are we, that few opportunities come our way to stand aside, perhaps only momentarily, to catch a glimpse of exactly how much relations between the genders are skewed.

I became more focused on this issue in 1969 when I directed our company of nine women and eight men in my own dramatic adaptation of T. S. Eliot's *Murder in the Cathedral,* which we performed in the sanctuary of San Francisco's Grace Cathedral on the 800th anniversary of Becket's martyrdom. It was my first major, large-scale directorial experience. To this day, I am still amazed at the foot-dragging I experienced from many of my male actors and the amount of time and energy required at the start of each evening's rehearsal to coax, cajole, and manipulate until most of them demonstrated a readiness to get down to work at last. At first it mystified me. Until that time, I had always viewed myself as a person; but here, I came to realize, I was being challenged, sometimes even overtly, as a woman. What did women know in general? And what on earth could they possibly know about directing a theater? Of course, my performers hadn't heard of Nuria Espert or Pina Bausch—Europeans had already begun to assign women a place in the cultural affairs of their countries.

By 1972-3, it became clear to me that I must embark on a theater work exploring gender expectation. During the two-year-long developmental period preceding performance of what came to be known as *After Eurydice* (i.e., after the destruction of the iconic woman, and/or Eurydice's version), we addressed the issues surrounding sexual role expectation through highly charged theatrical exercises designed to plumb the deeply unconscious gender assumptions of the company, again, divided equally between male and female performers.

I go into some detail here because, although clearly a company of nineteen performers can hardly be viewed as a statistical sampling, all were between the ages of eighteen and forty, and all were American-born with one exception (one of the men was Turkish). Some five or six months into rehearsal, the company became so intensely polarized along gender lines it could no longer function creatively. I arranged for a furlough, only to reconvene a year after the first rehearsals had begun, but with a company that had shed most of the previous season's artists.

Two improvisational series in particular support the thesis I want to propose here, namely that gender differences are unconscious, and until they become conscious, fundamentally irreconcilable. To understand our way of creating a dramatic work, some background in basic performance vocabulary is necessary. The first unit of our working language is sound and movement, wherein an actor proposes a full-bodied gesture and vocal production originating from impulse, repeats that sound and gesture in a chain of repetitions called a "locked action," eventually passing it on to a fellow artist who first mirrors it, and later transforms it into another locked action.

In a more complex exercise, a motor impulse might come from a circle of performers synchronizing their breath, leading to the emergence of a "conductor," one actor who, in sound and movement, might establish a world to which the other actors harmonize with their own variety of sounds and movements. (For a discussion of such an action, see Section 13, page 43.) Sounds might lead to pre-verbal and eventually into verbal expression in the form of the phrase, a charged series of words further illuminating the feelings being expressed—and repeated, as with the locked action. But, in all of this process, there is rarely any discussion or pre-planning; it is up to the director to provide instructions so sensitive their delineation allows the actors freedom to take the necessary risks, without overburdening them with too much specifying detail. Discussion follows the evening's series of (usually) three cumulatively layered improvisatory exercises.

In the process of building the piece itself, an exercise in two parts was conducted in dyads. The first series of dyads were same-sex. In each pair Man A initiated a locked action representing traditionally male work, usually a full-bodied movement, the kind that might accompany two men sawing a tree or digging a ditch; Man B mirrored; eventually Man B transformed Man A's locked action into different locked action representing another example of men's traditional physical work. Women did the same, but rather than digging ditches, they may have carded wool, or washed clothing.

The second part of the exercise paired the company in mixed-gender dyads. The instruction was for the men to teach their work to the women using sound and movement in a locked action; and to reverse at a certain point—for women to teach the men women's work. In the discussion following I asked the artists to talk about their feelings doing the work of the opposite gender. The women spoke first. They got right into the men's large-bodied movements and thoroughly relished them. They enjoyed the grunts, and pre-verbal curses, and expressed enthusiasm for their ability to dig and curse with the best of them. It came time for the men to register their feelings about participating in women's work. Whereas the women had become voluble almost to excess, the men expressed their enthusiasm for engaging in women's work with *total silence*.

Some days later, equipped now with their basic rehearsal vocabulary, I asked the company to form two same-gender teams. I asked each to create a "society" in which the work of men and women would be shared equally, and which would include a formal process of initiation by which the exercise would integrate the opposite gender. Because of its complexity, brief pre-discussion was allowed.

While the women remained spectators, the men chose to set up their activities in four quadrants, much like a playing field. The southwest corner was allocated to "work;" the northwest corner to "eating and drinking;" the northeast corner to "singing and dancing" (presumably because they had drunk to excess); and the southeast corner to "sleep." The most significant aspect however, of this "egalitarian" world was the center where the quadrants met and which functioned as a kind of initiation point, or *sipapu* (although the men were probably not aware of the role the womb of the world plays in Amerindian tradition). Here the women, who were grabbed by the arms and legs from the periphery of the space and hauled to the center, were positioned on a table—provided by the back of a male actor hunching on all fours—and literally banged up and down, until the male actor providing the table rolled out from under her body as a newly-born man. He was immediately put to work, and the woman was dragged off to the sleeping quarters and put to bed! In that evening's discussion, it became apparent that the men actually believed they had created an egalitarian world. Nothing would convince them otherwise, even though at a certain pass, some of the women had spontaneously revolted and stopped the exercise!

Despite the two full years our company devoted to gender-role exploration creating *After Eurydice*—and especially for one who thinks and construes the world in imagery—my full recognition of the weight of history and prehistory didn't come about until 1974 while accompanying my partner on a trip to Crete and Greece. We devoted a whole day to exploring the architecture of the Minoan palace at Knossos. Everywhere we roamed, on its terraces, and in its patios—granted Knossos has been heavily reconstructed—there is a feeling of airiness and freedom, as if the builders had designed an edifice which, offering shelter, shade, and quiet, at the same time let the world of nature in. Frescoes (copies of originals which can be found in museums in Athens and Heraklion) celebrated the many living things that the culture held dear: its vegetation, its flowers, its fish and dolphins, its shells, and its nubile young men and women. The terraces overlooking the countryside and the surrounding mountains were crenelated with bull's horns (emblemizing the female pubis), the emblem of the Goddess—for Crete partook of the Civilization of Old Europe, a civilization which enshrined the Great Goddess.

Days later we found ourselves near the Gulf of Corinth in mainland Greece, overlooking Mycene, the hilltop stronghold of Agamemnon, instigator with his brother, Menelaus, of the Trojan War. Already from that great distance I took its measure: the massive grey walls seemed more fortress than palace. There seemed to be no way to admit light. More than anything, the forbidding citadel evoked a sense of imprisonment, a feeling, which must have reflected and intensified the worldview of the men and women who once lived there.

Such disparity is reflected in the misogyny and unrelenting patriarchy of most of our present-day institutions. We see how they play themselves out in today's fragile world. Persistent efforts by the U.S. federal and state legislatures (predominantly male) to squelch women's abortion rights, and to close women's health clinics in thirty-five states, guaranteeing that women will no longer be able to find legal (not to mention safe) abortion providers, are a clear barometer of the degree to which misogyny is on the rise—as is racism—in the United States. And given the ascendency of the rule of corporatocracy both in the U.S. and globally, it comes as no surprise. An uncontrolled birthrate guarantees cheap labor where, to survive, people are forced to work in factories that occasionally have a nasty habit of burning to the ground; it favors the social conditions that result in mass imprisonment where prison labor has become the modern slavery; and it guarantees canon fodder for all the profitable war enterprises choking the Pentagon pipeline. It comes as no surprise that health insurance companies have denied coverage to women on the grounds that domestic violence and pregnancy are "pre-existing" conditions—which in the case of pregnancy has been pre-existing following the evolution of the platypus, when mammals gave up the habit of laying eggs.

In *Empire of Illusion*, Chris Hedges describes the role of pornography and its prevalence in the United States. He cites statistics. There are 13,000 porn films made every year in the United States. He cites worldwide porn revenues—with AT&T the biggest player—of $97 billion in 2006, more than the revenues of Microsoft, Google, Amazon, eBay, Yahoo!, Apple, Netflix and Earthlink combined! Hedges writes:

> Porn films are not about sex.... There is no acting because none of the women are permitted to have what amounts to

a personality. The one emotion they are allowed…is an unquenchable desire to satisfy men, especially if that desire involves the women's physical and emotional degradation…. It promotes masturbation…. [It's] about getting yourself off at someone else's expense.

Hedges writes about the permanent physical injuries women suffer to their orifices in exchange for money, and lots of it, but their careers ultimately leave them injured for life, addicted to drugs, and very often destitute. He quotes Robert Jensen, author of *Getting Off: Pornography and the End of Masculinity:*

> What does it say about our culture that cruelty is so easy to market? What is the difference between glorifying violence in war, and glorifying the violence of sexual domination…? We accept a culture flooded with images of women who are sexual commodities. Increasingly, women in pornography are not people having sex, but bodies upon which sexual activities of increasing cruelty are played out. And many men— maybe a majority of men—like it.

Today's news carries reports of a recent investigation among American-born males between the ages of fourteen and twenty-one. Among them, four percent admitted to having raped women.

The same men who may profess love for individual women seek to subjugate, control, and denigrate them by suppressing women's rights. Their public stances play out in the global arena in the form of laws and economic pressures that adversely affect the lives of women the world over by, for example, denying them agricultural assistance in favor of male beneficiaries, although at least 80 percent of food production throughout the world is performed by women; by denying women birth control as a condition of foreign aid; by limiting educational opportunities for women, although education has been proved to be the most effective means of counteracting overpopulation; and by waging wars and covert interventions where civilian casualties are, the majority of them, women and their children. Of all the animals, only the human primate—and the chimpanzee—bear intense hostility to female members of their own species. No other animal behavior shows a similar pattern of gender-based power relations.

In *Sex, Time and Power*, Shlain describes how various disciplines have attempted to explain this uniquely primate behavior. He points to the Western canon, a literature enshrining the works of mostly white males, from Isaiah, Plato, Augustine, Bacon, Luther and Calvin through the Enlightenment, eventually to include Nietzche, Marx, Hegel, and Freud, to name a very few. None of these later champions of human rights seemed to have thought it was important to free women from their roles as servants. Religious figures such as Jesus, Muhammad and Lao Tzu, despite their being well disposed towards women, saw their teachings co-opted by male disciples who lost no time laying down patriarchal law.

Some anthropologists propose that while men are associated with the predominating culture, women are associated with nature in view of their proximity to birth, to monthly bleeding, breastfeeding, and discharge of body fluids. Historically and traditionally men have ascribed the most remarkable and malevolent attributes to menstrual blood but apparently not to bloodshed on the battlefield. Because of their physiology, women acquired an inseparable association in men's minds with the chthonic, with life and death; in their subconscious minds men saw Woman as a force of nature, and Western men's association with nature has predominantly been to attempt its domination. Other anthropologists suggest that having acquired control over literacy and the symbol-generating authority of language, men became the originators of laws, religions and other social institutions, to the detriment of women. Sara Robinson expands on these ideas when she makes the connection between misogyny and what motivates patriarchal men to be terrified of birth control. By defining women in terms of biological destiny, that is, by insisting that women were born to bear children, and that they had no other life options, men "thrived":

The ego candy they feasted on by virtue of automatically outranking half the world's population was only the start of it. They got full economic and social control over our bodies, our labor, our affections, and our futures. They got to make the rules, name the gods we would worship, and dictate the terms we would live under. In most cultures, they had the right to sex on demand within the marriage, and also to break their marriage vows with impunity—a luxury that would get women banished or killed. As long as pregnancy remained the defining fact of our lives, they got to run the whole show. The world was their party, and they had a fabulous time.

Western psychoanalytic theory proposes that for boys to become men, they must repudiate their ties to their mothers. Existential philosophy—in the person of Simone de Beauvoir—advanced the hypothesis that it was hunting which predisposed men to become dominant because of its attendant thrills and dangers in contrast to women, whose work, although more enduring, might be viewed as less flamboyant.

Physiologists attribute the burdens of patriarchy and misogyny to testosterone, a hormone that builds muscle mass, strength, and stamina, but fuels aggression. Men have as much as ten times more of it than women do. According to Shlain, it shapes men's attitudes toward the weak and timid not just because it makes them want to dominate those around them, but, because, in my view, they fear weakness and timidity in themselves. Shlain, who is a highly trained laparoscopic surgeon, cites statistics showing that men's testosterone levels correlate with their attitude towards women. Men with high levels marry less frequently, and are more likely to become abusive when they do.

There is yet another factor about which, as a former theater-maker, I have been speculating for some time. The pitch of women's voices (which is largely culturally determined) may tend to disempower them because all too often it lends their voices the timbre of children's voices, as is becoming increasingly the case in the United States where female pitch creeps higher year by year, with more and more introjection of hesitating place holders (such as 'like'), and upspeak (where sentences meant to be declarative end in a higher-pitched question mark).

Some time ago, Roy Hart, a French theater artist, developed an artistic programme which attempted to bridge the conscious with the unconscious aspects of the psyche between male and female, between feeling and intellect, and between what he called the dark and the light aspects of the personality. His work with the human voice grew out of the discoveries of Alfred Wolfson, who believed that the human voice is not solely the output of anatomical components, but the expression of the entire personality. His premise was that it was possible, by tapping the full gamut of an individual's vocal resonators, to develop a fuller range not just of sound but of personally accessible emotion. Reportedly, audiences who observed Roy Hart's actors in performance sometimes came away feeling deeply unsettled, especially when they perceived women speaking in a man's voice; and conversely, men speaking in a woman's voice.

Blanca Bosker, writing for the *Huffington Post*, reported a feature of Apple's Siri "which makes 'her' appear *more capable*" [itals added]. She quotes Stanford Professor Clifford Nass, whose research shows that people apply gender biases even to digital voices: "Female voices are seen, on average, as less intelligent than male voices.... Men and women not only sound different when they speak, but typically employ different terms and words." According to Nass, men specify ('two,' 'five'); women equivocate ('some,' 'often'). The article concludes by claiming that "personal avatars with female voices can be viewed as less knowledgeable but they are preferred...*in helper or assistant roles* [itals. added]."

Louann Brisendine, whose work I tend to want to discount because of its extremely narrow cultural, virtually valley-girl slant, claims that in matters of courtship and marriage, males favor women whose voices are high-pitched. Much of the literature I see, particularly as it refers to matters of gender, assumes very circumscribed cultural biases, but Bosker's very brief article points to a much broader assumption:

In other roles—and other countries—female voices may not fly at all. In *The Man Who Lied to His Laptop*, Nass documents how BMW was forced to recall one of its cars because male drivers in Germany didn't trust the female voice offering directions from the car's navigation system. In Japan, a call center operated by Fidelity would rely on an automated female voice to give stock quotes, but would transfer customers to an automated male voice for transactions.

Pitch neutrality is another of many attributes primates began to lose when they developed speech. And if, as Wolfson and Hart believed, the human voice is the expression of the underlying psyche and not just a physical production, we might infer that in the contemporary world *both* genders have permitted themselves to be boxed into hardened roles, which act to polarize and isolate them from each other.

28. Nailing the Connections

Why is the relationship between genders significant in attempting to address the problems of our increasingly dystopic world? And what role does acceptance of their assigned power relations by the genders play in the dynamic of that world?

Assumption of power roles by women only keeps increasing. Many more women activists have made their voices heard of late—a few of them admittedly at higher than optimal vocal pitches: Vandana Shiva, Mairead Maquire, Cindy Sheehan, Carol Urner, Medea Benjamin, Hattie Nestel, the late Barbara George, Cynthia McKinney, Megan Rice, Granny D, Sherry Ott, Dianne Wilson, Charmaine White Face, Helen Caldicott, Elizabeth Warren, Cindy Folkers, Kendra Ulrich, Wendy Davis, Arundhati Roy, Kathy Kelley, the late Wangari Maahtai, Dolores Huerta, Eileen Myoko Smith, not to mention all the Japanese women of the Fukushima 100, to name only a very few. Rebellions are now being led by indigenous matriarchs the world over.

More women are regaining their lost voices, and predictably, that very fact has caused those in the halls of power—a few of them women—to collaborate, taking counteractive measures such as militarizing police forces, and supporting secrecy, surveillance, harassment, and increasing incarceration. But polarization between those in power and those in active resistance clearly shows significant gender imbalance.

Although power lines are no longer drawn—in the contemporary world at least—exclusively along gender lines, the continuing imbalance is what merits notice. The victims of global war are disproportionally women and their children. A rigged global food distribution that causes regional famine targets mostly women and their children. The economic structure of wage distribution primarily targets women, and the allocation of welfare the world over is prejudicial against women and their children. The public pension systems of many industrialized countries, especially that of the United States, are structured so as to be actuarially unfair to women who live longer than men, but who earn less during their working lives. We can generalize here that in all economic sectors, the world's most severe and chronic poverty disproportionately affects women. We can also generalize here that institutions which uphold this antiquated system are primarily powered by men. We could speculate that dis-empowered women, had they ever been consulted, would have drawn on a completely other-directed worldview, prompting them to consider alternative organizational possibilities built along more collaborative lines. But, so far, such a notion remains speculative.

Looking now at the demography of protest and resistance, even excluding such women-directed coalitions as Code Pink, Mothers for Peace, and Women's International League for Peace and Freedom, women activists still seem consistently to outnumber men among those protesting at School of the Americas, America's torture academy for foreign-born nationals; at military bases from which drones are launched; at Vandenberg against missile launchings toward the Kwajaleins, where depleted uranium is used for ballast; at reactor gates; at foreclosure hearings; and in the actual halls and chambers of government. (But not consistently. "Democracy Now" featured heroic postman, Doug Hughes, landing a gyrocopter on the Capitol lawn to deliver 533 letters to all members of Congress calling for an end to private money in election campaigns. http://www.commondreams.org/views/2015/05/15/can-gyrocopter-gang-start-political-reform-movement).

But for the most part, activist movements still seem to be peopled primarily by women. Yet there must be equal numbers of men who desperately oppose the use of nuclear energy, fracking, mountaintop removal, assassination-by-drone, but the reasons their presence is not yet fully manifest are not entirely evident. We can speculate as to why this trend seems to continue. Assuming it's because men still occupy the role of breadwinner, and that their economic commitments prevent participation, would be wrong. Men are no longer primary breadwinners. And where are the retired men whose time is far less structured? On the other hand, we *can* speculate that in contrast to men, women, *because of their inferior economic status,* have much less left to lose.

Yet in my view, we need to look beyond mere economics. The human womb is still assigned to women, a fact not likely to change any time soon. All women share in its griefs and pleasures. It cushions the placenta in pregnancy. It is the strongest muscle in the human body, without which giving birth is not possible. As such, whether we will or no, we are the continuation of the species. Without our collaboration, the species dies out. We bleed. We tend to begin sometimes as early at 10 years of age, and end sometime into our fifties. Clocked to the phases of the moon, these bloodlettings are our internal calendar. The sight of blood emanating from our bodies during the course of our reproductive decades, must imprint us in many ways. It reminds us every month of the body's fragility and its mortality. It allows us to imagine the horror of those male-centered battlefield blood lettings more easily. Although there are any number of examples where in one manner or another, women refuse the nurturing roles of motherhood, the habit of nurture, ingrained culturally, and prompted biologically by childbearing and lactation, tends to foster in the personality an intensified concern for others and for assuming helping roles in the larger society. In my twelve years directing a theater company, I had ample opportunity to observe that, undoubtedly because of differences in their cultural upbringing, women in general are far more emotionally available than men.

Although more and more, especially in desperate economic times, we see amongst brutalized women refusal of the parental role, the great majority of women who bear life nurture it, often in the face of great hardship. As women give birth, they are born anew into time, the future time of their children. It is that expanded sense of time that lends them their powers of empathy for the vulnerable and the disadvantaged. Past their bearing years, old women, childless or otherwise, often play out their impulses to nurture by cosseting their pets, and overwatering their plants. In some women the need to nurture encompasses the landscape, even extending in some cases to the whole planet. I count people like Helen Caldicott, Rachel Carson, Vandana Shiva, and Wangari Maahtai part of that blessed company.

Beyond the more obvious considerations, women demonstrate many characteristics of their oppressed class. As with all generalization, a spectrum exists, and there are notorious exceptions, women like Hillary Clinton, Victoria Nuland, Margaret Thatcher, Madeleine Albright, Diane Feinstein, Condolezza Rice, Lady Barbara Judge, Yulia Tymoshenko, and Indira Gandhi, who see their advantage in espousing the male-privileged powers bestowed by hierarchy. But by and large, the behavior of women in terms of their use of language as a means of lending one another mutual support* and their heightened sense of gender solidarity parallels that of oppressed classes the world over.

But aside from considerations of biology and of women's status in the world, at play in the displacement of the female Great Goddess by the male sky god of the Kurgans is the radical shift in the West's views not only of gender equality but of the sacred. It

---

* Welsh even has a word for it: *furan.*

has been assumed by some that mankind's passage from pastoralism to agriculture sets the stage for the competition for resources that capitalism implies (although the pre-history of Old Europe suggests it was more of a two-way street). But the means towards expansionism has shifted from outright warfare and mayhem to more sophisticated forms. Increasingly the "law" and those who write and "interpret" it play a determining role. North Africans who had tilled the soil from time immemorial had their land seized by French colonizers on the pretext they were unable to produce land titles, titles which historically they had never held. Similarly with Native Americans. And, in a bow to colonialism, the neocolonial "new world order's" secretive trade "agreements," drawn up by an oligarchy behind closed doors, facilitate land grabs and resource extraction from disempowered people throughout the world.

Traditionally by contrast, indigenous relationship to the soil has been inverse in the sense that people belong to the Earth, not the other way round. Land was not something that could be owned or sold, any more than you could sell your mother because the Earth was sacred—*Wakan,* according to the Lakota Sioux and the Mexica of Teotihuacan. In a world where all things were seen as interconnected, the sacred in the essence of the soil itself extended to all things which came from the soil.

In 1981, I travelled many hundreds of miles in North Africa, occasionally living with Berber families—in houses, sometimes in tents—who would not hear of my staying in a hotel, and who insisted on offering me their generous hospitality. I stayed in small towns where five times a day, no matter where I might find myself, I heard the voice of the muezzin broadcasting the call for prayer. In the Morocco of 1981, Islam was the sacred glue, which, with its rules of mutuality and despite pockets of desperate poverty, held the society together in some kind of harmony.

Eight years later, I travelled some 3,000 miles in India. Wherever I ventured, in temples, obviously, but also in the most humble of dwellings, in food stalls, and restaurants, in shops, in recital halls, in concert auditoriums, always there was a shrine, a votive candle or incense stick burning with offerings of flowers and fruits; before every concert, every dance recital, every raga recital, performers offered a prayer to some deity. They prayed to honor a god, not to ask for favors. Often they played in a state of trance, the trance that comes from a variety of religious ecstasy. Many aspects of Hindu life were conducted in an atmosphere of prayer. Many moments seemed to be felt as sacred. Even animals shared in that sense of sacredness. One dawn, in Madurai, I witnessed a group of women making offerings and bowing to a temple elephant.

In the once-country of Iraq, the iconic spiral ziggurat at Samarra emblemizes a religious outlook utterly different from that of the West. Westerners assume that its spiral shape reaches up to heaven for mankind to get closer to the Godhead to raise his voice in supplication. Quite the contrary: it is a convenient ramp for God to descend and dwell among mankind on Earth! Balaji is the folk name for the Hindu god Venkateswara. He is the city of Tirupati's god of poor people. His effigy stands on my living room side table: made of purple heartwood, he bears a mustache, he has lost his breasts, but his hips still round with the fullness they once had, because long ago, before history, Balaji was a woman. This god, too, shows a tendency to fraternize; he/she is the people's god, not one to be worshipped from afar. Legend has it that rather than allowing the humble and downtrodden to behold his divinity from eyes that would blast them with their radiance were they to gaze at him directly, he comes to the poor blind, his eyes dimmed—and compassionate.

From the archeological evidence, I infer with Gimbutas that that is how life in Old Europe must have been lived, in daily presence of the sacred, of the Goddess of the Earth who gives life and takes it away, and who emblemizes rebirth, whether represented in the form of a bird, serpent, moth, or a metamorphosing butterfly.

Birth, life, death, and rebirth were coded in the form of spirals figuring on objects, some of them as humble as food jars and cooking vessels. And many of the small, palm-sized goddess figurines are covered with deeply incised patterns of parallel marks that resonate with landscape patterns made by strip agriculture cultivation of the soils, thereby associating the sacred both with the physical body and with the Earth itself, and confirming both landscape and body as sacred.

Is it appropriate therefore to conclude that a matrilineal civilization founded on worship of the Great Goddess must always have been peaceful, free of strife? In the human story, relying on generalities is dangerous if not impossible. In ancient Celtic civilization women warriors fought as fiercely as men. In general, territory was the expansionist ground where war, mayhem, and greed played themselves out, regardless of whether a civilization was nomadic, or agriculturally based. Are women more open to recognizing the sacredness of life? Does it mean that the only peace in the world is to be had among the creatures of the seas? Does it come as coincidence that all cetacean societies are matrilineal? What is the connection?

In an article on the relationship of gender to environmental outlook, David Roberts summarizes recent social science research. Although women's socialization may count as a factor, Roberts concludes that women—and all other minorities—assess risk differently from white males. He refers to a study showing that "the differences in risk perception [are] almost entirely a function of 'identity-protective-cognition.'" And quoting a 1994 study, he amplifies this idea: "Perhaps white males see less risk in the world because they create, manage, control, and benefit from so much of it. [Others] see the world as more dangerous because they are more vulnerable..., they benefit less from its technologies and institutions, and [enjoy] less power and control."

29. Language Creep and Language Bleed

In *Sexes à travers les languages*, Luce Irigaray, the French feminist philosopher, observes:

> The world is changing…. With its emphasis on money, its survival seems at risk, its condition destructive of our value system and unsupportive of life itself…. Those means of communication established exclusively by patriarchal systems may very well stifle or destroy ways of interaction more suited to…the necessities of actual living. Feminine consciousness is not only essential for reproduction but for the preservation of life and of culture itself. Ultimately the question at hand comes down to whether our civilization is still hell bent on declaring the female gender like some kind of ugly blemish… or a hold over from a previous animal nature, or whether indeed it might lend itself at last to the salvation of human culture. If such a change comes about it will be by re-sexualizing language itself….

Irigaray's immense learning notwithstanding, we cannot deliberately change our languages, let alone re-sexualize them, whether German, English, Spanish or otherwise. Mandating a name change such as "freedom" fries for French fries because we're miffed at the French for refusing to join the "coalition of the willing" exemplifies an imposed attempt to change a language, and as such, the change can never stick.

Yet, if we pay attention, we notice that since its first stirrings more than fifty years ago, the Women's Movement has come to be reflected in a shift in the customary use of American English. We tend to by-pass the singular possessive pronoun in favor of a distinctly a-grammatical usage. Here is an example from a recent e-mail: "We should fix the system so that if *a doctor* was consulted on you, *they* should show up in your drop down menu of doctors to e-mail." This sentence avoids the awkward, politically correct use of *he* or *she,* or just the male-privileging *he.* Linguistic examples of this kind of organic (i.e. non-deliberate) bending of traditional grammatical rules to reflect cultural change I refer to as "language creep." It reflects, as in the above example, welcome change in current views of the world; at the same time, it may be seen to reflect the vagaries of history.

I believe that we must become more aware of the language we use so automatically that words come tumbling from our mouths with hardly any forethought. We need to begin noticing the extensive metaphoric invasion of our language by militaristic word choices. Do we really want congress to *target* Social Security? Do I really want to *shoot* you an e-mail? Do I want to *fire off* a letter? Do I hope my play won't *bomb?* Do I anticipate Harry Reid will choose the *nuclear option?* Do I expect George Galloway to go *ballistic?* Do you plan to *blow* your mother-in-law *off?* Which do you prefer, *bullet* points, or dingbats? Maybe you don't want to be *blown away* by the Disney industry's latest cultural artifact. Maybe you prefer not to *waste* another *camel jockey.* And you hope no one gives you any *flak.*

In her article "Slick'ems, Glick'ems, Christmas Trees and Cookie Cutters: Nuclear Language and How We Learned to Pat the Bomb," appearing in the 1987 *Bulletin of Atomic Scientists,* Carol Cohn points to a number of hierarchical uses of jargon to establish the in-ness of the "in" group, and to distinguish it from the "out" group, employed by institutions and entities as disparate as the military on the one hand, and the academy on the other—the academy which favors opacity on the grounds that if a subject acquires a sufficiently arcane aura, it must be important enough to obtain grant support. Even the Crips and Bloods have their own jargon—a full set of "grilles" refers to gold-encased front teeth—and one language at least, Caló, the *lingua franca* of the Iberian Romani people, is kept from outsiders to maintain the Rom as separate. She identifies such in-groups as discourse communities. And she points to what I call language bleed, that is, the use of homey expressions to domesticate terror. She gives chilling examples: Nuclear missiles on board U.S. submarines are referred to as "Christmas trees." Their targets are referred to as "home addresses."

The 2004 publication of John Perkins' *Confessions of an Economic Hit Man* made it clear that the U.S. government conducts its wars, both domestic and foreign, on the economic as well as the military front. In business school, tactics and strategy are taught using the U.S. Marine Corps doctrinal manuals. And as military language and metaphors cycle into civilian life, so civilian life reflects the military in such topical matters as Presidential "campaigns," where headquarters are referred to as the "war room." Likewise, civilian sport metaphors creep into military campaign reports so that in 1991, a Desert Storm tank maneuver was termed a "Hail Mary pass." That war's "shock and awe" opening was termed a "kickoff."

Once we become aware of how deeply culture affects word choice, and how word choice perpetuates worldview, we begin to notice how militarism plays itself out in the words we hear on entertainment-as-news; and what we see when we watch Hollywood's factory products or attend the Super Bowl. Once aware, we can decide whether our speech might benefit from alternative word choices—and we may decide the boycott is the best response to Hollywood and the TV infomercials that pass for news, especially since the real news is much more accessible via the internet. Making our own determinations may in turn alert us to the degree to which our culture reflects militarism in other aspects such as sports, fashion, and toy design, and, once aware how increasingly militaristic it continues to become, we may be inclined to find very creative ways to push actively against the trend.

How language is used by individuals to assert their dominance through usage, choice of affect, tone, or level of discourse also speaks to power relations. These revolve around the more deeply embedded structures in a language by which it mediates the tenor of interpersonal relations, how it sees the individual (as sole and separate agent or as a member of the "we"); how it addresses the individual; how it makes provision—or not—for diffidence, and discretion; how it sets up the kind of protective space around others which prevents invasion of their integrity and privacy, and allows them the dignity of personal autonomy. For example, you may want to encourage a student or subordinate by using the word, "Good!" But in Japanese, you can't avail yourself of this usage because it's seen as too aggressive, too invasive of another's personal integrity. Rather you have to assert that in your judgment, *you* think something is good. You take responsibility for your judgment, mediated by your ownership of it, and thus remove your speech from the arena of dominant power relations. Call it respect, call it reverence. Call it deep listening if you will. It is one of the main areas where language and culture intersect.

These considerations touch on what American psychiatric practice refers to as "boundaries," namely the space of respect that exists between autonomous individuals, perhaps because in our culture we have no explicit linguistically embedded ways of honoring the integrity of the individuals we deal with in daily life, including those near and dear to us of whom we do not wish to take advantage. One of the ways of establishing and upholding personal "boundaries" is use of the "I-statement," an idea which dates from the '60s when it was first popularized by Thomas Gordon as part of his play therapy work with children. Its effectiveness consists in deflecting the placing of blame on another person; instead, the speaker takes full responsibility for the ownership of his or her feelings. For example, one may replace, "You always interrupt when someone is talking," with, "I don't like it when I am interrupted," or better still, "I would like to listen to what so-and-so is saying," or even more telling, "Could we please listen to what so-and-so is saying?"

This concept, a very obvious one, lies at the root of conflict resolution. Because the languages of the West, especially American English, are poor in the deeply embedded structures that support deep respect, the least we can do is compensate by adopting these rather elementary principles.

30. Triumphs of Western Civilization

When Mohandas Gandhi was asked what he thought of Western Civilization, he observed that he thought it might be a good idea.

Consider the historical trajectory of so-called Western civilization, a civilization almost entirely articulated by Proto-Indo-European-derived languages, beginning with the Age of Heresy, including such religious massacres as that of the Cathars, or of the Huguenots; or the depredations of the Inquisition against Jews, Muslims, and so-called heretics; or of the Crusades against the Islamic World, a conflict that still plays itself out in today's Middle East. Consider the so-called Age of "Discovery," during which expeditions sponsored by European monarchs set sail for the New World to a history of plunder (for territory, gold, silver, and slaves); massacres and mass displacement of indigenous people such as the Taino (reduced by Columbus in his position as viceroy of Hispaniola from eight million in 1500 to 22,000 survivors by 1542*); and the genocidal campaigns waged against the North and South American Indians including the Aztecs and the Maya. Consider the Age of Conquest, when Spain, France, England, and many other smaller European countries fought each other and vied for spoils in such countries as Australia, New Zealand, Indonesia, Canada, and India, and later carved up Africa and the Middle East.

Consider religion, which until the Protestant Reformation held a man being tortured and put to death as its central icon, and maintained a devout predisposition to treat women as chattel. Consider the later Age of Colonization which reduced the native population of continental North America from 12,000,000 before contact to 237,000 by 1900.* Consider that repeated examples show that the Cross of Christianity preceded—or followed—the

---

*Ward Churchill: *Indians Are Us: Culture and Genocide in native North America*

Sword. Consider that with the Reformation, Protestantism, the new religion, encouraged its followers to overlook good works, to dispense with a sense of obligation to one's fellow beings, enshrining faith and faith alone. Consider the epidemic of witch burning that swept over Europe from the fourteenth to the end of the eighteenth century.

Consider that the American Colonies were the first to overthrow their English yoke in the American Revolution of 1776, followed by the Venezuelan War of Independence (1810-1823), whereas African people colonized by the Dutch, the English, the Germans, French, Spanish, Belgians, and Latvians, didn't begin succeeding at the same game until well into the 20th century, nearly 300 years later, perhaps—we might speculate—it might have been because the North American and Latin American colonists were descended from speakers of the very same language, born of the very same stock that colonized these countries in the first place.

Consider the three-centuries-long subjugation of nearly half the world's people by the British Empire. Consider the horrors of German Nazism during the Second World War. Consider the post-World War II financial arrangements codified at Bretton-Woods. Consider the current age of Neo-colonialism and its resource-grabbing, particularly in countries such as now-partitioned Sudan, where we can actually see the mechanisms of genocide at work much as it has been practiced throughout history, but now under the scrutiny of Hubert Sauper's relentlessly probing camera in his Sundance-awarded, "We Come As Friends." Consider further that the New World Order, the globalized system now enveloping the world in new forms of slavery, global dominance, and ecological devastation—and the UN and NATO, for that matter—have been organized predominantly by Western, and Western-born agents. Consider and group together all the post-World-War II regional conflagrations we have yet to recognize as World War III.

If we consider all these things, we begin to see history in very broad strokes as relentlessly expansionist, exploitative, and violent, a history driven by supremacist peoples whose social and political organization originates in patriarchy, violence, warfare, and elitist power relations. It is the history of predators who happen to speak disparate Proto-Indo-European-derived tongues. The four exceptions, that is, European languages other than PIE-derived, namely Finnish, Hungarian, Basque, and Estonian, are spoken by people who also happen to have participated in less "successful" attempts at colonization, despite (with the exception of Hungary) their advantaged position on the littorals, positions which may very well have offered a strong competitive influence in the first place.

31. The Insurrection of Subjugated Knowledges

For the last ten or fifteen years, the[re has been] immense and proliferating criticizability of things, institutions, practices, and discourses.... But alongside this crumbling the facts were also revealing something.... Beneath this whole thematic, through it and even within it, we have seen what might be called the insurrection of subjugated knowledges.

—Foucault, writing in *Society Must Be Defended*, 1976

In the arena of European thought, Structuralism, a critical philosophy which determined that cultural production is unambiguous and fixed in its meanings, gave way to Post-Structuralism, which took as its goal the deconstruction of all meanings previously construed as fixed. Old concepts and political alignments came up for grabs. The women's movement drew parallels with the movement for racial liberation. The politics of opposition to colonialist wars in countries like Vietnam made common cause with movements for national liberation in Africa and in South America. The world had begun to wake up from the long European nightmare induced by its Proto-Indo-European-derived hierarchical world view.

Already in 1961, the great apologist of liberation movements, Franz Fanon, was working in North Africa. Fanon was a psychiatrist whose service in Algeria allowed him to witness Algeria's war of independence against French colonialism and its sanction of torture practices in that same war. Here is Fanon writing in *The Wretched of the Earth*:

> That same Europe where they were never done talking of Man, and where they never stopped proclaiming that they were only anxious for the welfare of Man: today we know with what sufferings humanity has paid for every one of their triumphs of the mind.... When I search for Man in the technique and the style of Europe, I see only a succession of negations of Man and an avalanche of murders.

Nor does Fanon allow the United States to escape his condemnation:

> Two centuries ago a former European colony decided to catch up with Europe. It succeeded so well that the United States of America became a monster, in which the taints, the sickness, and the inhumanity of Europe have grown to appalling dimensions.
>
> So comrades, let us not pay tribute to Europe by creating states, institutions, and societies which draw their inspiration from her.... Humanity is waiting for something from us other than such an...obscene caricature.

In Berkeley the vast demonstrations of the Free Speech Movement of 1964-65 and the massive student opposition to the war in Vietnam sounded the prelude to 1968, the iconic year which marks the point where Eurocentrism and its millennia-old assumptions palpably began to fall apart. All the strict Structuralist meanings of the West—hegemony, colonialism, imperialism, racism, and subjugation of women—converged in the crescendo of the student opposition movement that ignited Paris in 1968, and which spread to the United States a year later in the longest student strike in American history, at San Francisco State University.

The degree to which the West has responded with intensifying and brutal opposition—covertly, by targeted assassination, as well as militarily and by means of ruthless economic warfare—reflects in part the measure of the strength and durability of these movements of liberation and this coalescence of movements. To cite only a few recent examples of that response: the Cuba twitter destabilization project; the subversion of the Bolivarian revolution in Venezuela by covert infiltration; the subversion of the Ukraine using covert operatives to foment unrest and institute a coup ousting the Ukraine's democratically elected, if corrupt, president; the covert destabilization of Libya, and assassination of former U.S. ally, Muhammad Gaddafi. These tactics go back as far and farther with the covert assassination in 1961 of Patrice Lumumba, one of Africa's first democratically elected leaders; the complicity of the CIA in Nelson Mandela's 27 years of imprisonment; the overthrow of democratically elected Jacobo Árbenz in Nicaragua; the ouster of democratically elected socialist president Salvador Allende in the CIA-backed Chilean coup of September 11, 1973; the subversion of the democratically-elected Aristede government in Haiti; and the re-emergence of Apartheid in the State of Israel with full U.S. sanction and support, to cite a very few examples.

Notwithstanding the constant struggle to sustain them, the gains of popular movements in such areas as education, health care, and agrarian reform continue to demonstrate models that a better world is possible. In Batista's pre-revolutionary Cuba for example, only one rural hospital existed; 60 percent of the population, although predominantly rural, was undernourished, and 80 percent of children had intestinal parasites, at that time the number one cause of death. Indoor plumbing was nearly non-existent. Half of Cuba's children did not attend school. Illiteracy in the countryside was 46 percent; among city-dwellers, 11 percent. Within one year (1961), as a result of a year-long effort to abolish illiteracy, Cuba was able to raise its level of literacy to 96 percent. (By contrast, 88 percent of the population in French colonialist Algeria was illiterate.)

Even before the Cuban war of revolution was over, rural hospitals and medical posts had been established. Within one year after the overthrow of the Batista dictatorship, all of Cuba's children were enrolled in school; 150,000 landless peasants had received subsistence lands; educational reform and infrastructure improvements had spread into remote areas. The rural medical service was staffed by recent graduates who undertook to volunteer for fixed periods, eventually resulting in a significant reduction in infant mortality and increase in life expectancy. And perhaps, what is most commendable, especially in the light of the mortality experienced in the U.S. among the Black population of New Orleans during the Katrina hurricane, Cuba's hurricane preparedness plans have resulted in keeping deaths from the sixteen storms that have swept Cuba from 2001 to 2012 to only 35.*

In an article titled "The Crime of Peaceful Protest," Chris Hedges had this to say: "The corporate state, which has proved utterly incapable of addressing the grievances and injustices endured by the underclass, is extremely nervous about the mass [Occupy] movements that have swept the [U.S.] in recent years. And if protests erupt again—as I think they will—the state hopes it will have neutralized much of the potential leadership."

What is telling, in my view, is that repression of movements designed to better the human condition continue to be met with consistently implacable opposition by the West, in particular the United States by medium of its foreign and domestic policies. There seems to be a punitive streak running through the larger oppression which resonates with the Puritan ethic underlying the foundation of this country and that believes that the vulnerable *are* undeserving because if they were deserving, they wouldn't belong to the vulnerable class in the first place. And they would have the means to defend themselves in court.

---

*Immediately following the U.S. experience of Katrina's devastation, the government of Cuba offered to send medical and paramedical units trained to protect vulnerable regions. The "Mission Accomplished" U.S. president of the moment refused.

32. Do-Si-Do: One Step Forward, Two Steps Back*

In human affairs, the Paleolithic is the dawning period where art and, possibly related, formal burial practices begin. Kathleen Jamie, writing in the September/October 2013 issue of *Orion Magazine*, describes a recent exhibition at the British Museum which included figurines, some only four centimeters long, of large-breasted and full hipped women; humanoid figures carved from bone with heads of animals; a tibia carved with the figures of two swimming reindeer, all carved by people who still lived in caves, and who wore tightly sewn skins to keep them warm in an age of retreating ice.

> Never before have [such] artworks from across Europe been assembled thus. I've heard that some people leave this exhibition in tears. I imagine they cry because they feel a deep sense of loss, even homesickness: we were Paleolithic for a long time. We have lost the animals' company. And perhaps people cry because they feel that we have not only forgotten, but been deluded, cheated out of our own ancient human history and self-knowledge. This exhibition identifies the beginning of our knowledge that we are like animals, and also, we are not like them.... Ice Age Art stops us short, and we go back out into the street asking—what have we become?

The journey of human primates has been long and arduous. Its triumphs have disguised increasingly catastrophic dangers. At almost all of its turning points, technology has been developed at the expense of sustainability, where a misguided sense of vision favors so-called progress, unlimited expansion, endless economic growth, and uninhibited controls: all these thresholds mark the geometrically accelerating evolution of the human path. With each step, we have moved closer to our own demise by fouling our own nest, and along with it, the habitat of all other beings on the earth.

---

* From Spanish: dos a dos, two by two.

In vain we hanker for what could not be. Like Koestler's dinosaurs, we can't get on our knees to beg for a second chance. Nor can we make it up to the creatures—including those of our own kind—we have wantonly sickened, displaced, and allowed to pass into extinction. We cannot offer anything that might pass for an apology without resorting to barefaced cynicism and abject hypocrisy.

Humanity may find some pockets on this planet where time is not yet measured in terms of progress, production and profit; where, rather than in terms of striving, it is defined in terms of listening to the voice of nature on a planet with the potential—unrecognized for eons—of becoming our very own garden of paradise, harboring the living of all its creatures in a balance, not necessarily of convenience, happiness or even harmony, but in terms of "fit."

V.

ON THE CONNECTEDNESS OF THINGS

33. Return to the Sea of Dreams

The place of my birth did not yield me the monumental landscapes of the Alps from where my mother hailed, and which, as
an adventuresome young woman she had climbed in hob-nailed
boots, roped to a long string of other climbers. I could never
imagine a terrestrial landscape less impoverished than my own
treeless streets and canyons of concrete—grey and unbroken by
sunlight except at noon. I could not imagine a forest. My few
trees were scrawny, imprisoned in spiked iron cages, or bursting
unruly through broken concrete sidewalks. I played in a field of
coal cinders, collecting them, scooping them up into my mother's discarded cold cream jars, and screwing the black caps over
them.

But from the time I first saw them at the age of four, the
blown glass diatoms and the deep-ocean diorama at New York
City's Museum of Natural History fired my imagination, which
is why, as a little girl, I reveled in the story of *The Five Chinese
Brothers*—stereotypical, bloodthirsty and sadistic as it was—because the third Chinese brother could swallow the ocean (which
he had to do to prevent being executed by drowning). I began to
imagine playing on the floors of the sea, but unencumbered by the
massive diving suit and helmet depicted in the museum diorama,
and freed of the breathing tube that leashed the diver to Earth's
atmosphere. I imagined a pristine world under the sea, uncluttered
by the mounting detritus of civilization: tin cans, old refrigerators,
crushed automobiles, downed aircraft, and ships that foundered
at sea. In the sea of my imaginings, I walked in riotously colored
gardens of sea slugs, sea cucumbers, and corrals, with showers of
silvery fish shot with colors of the rainbow. Immune to all harm
and danger, I picked bouquets of sea anemones whose hallucinatory tentacles would, flower-like, remain open to the eternity
of my gaze. I dreamed myself weightless, moving with the easy
and unconscious grace of fish. I scaled the steep cliffs of the
continental shelf, coming eye to eye with serpent-like electric

eels, impervious to their paralyzing sting.

From the time *Pinocchio* was first read to me, and when I first heard the tale of Jonah and the whale, I wondered what living within a whale's belly might feel like. Still adorning my walls to this day is a Persian depiction of an angel offering the prophet a shirt to clothe his nakedness when he emerges fetus-like from the maw of what looks like a gigantic carp. But I shook and shuddered and turned blue with fright when my father first carried me out into the waves, nearly to be sucked down by the undertow. Perhaps it was then that I stopped imagining living beneath the waves. But observing their blue-green translucence, hearing the chatter of foam receding with the tides, my sense of wonder never ceased. I marveled at my first discovery of the trilobite-like carcass of a horseshoe crab; I thrilled at finding the desiccated skeleton of a tiny sea horse, which I kept in my child's treasury along with brightly colored pebbles, shells, and the fiery wings of monarch butterflies. This was my child's small Garden of Eden.

Once, at the age of six, I accompanied my parents and their friends to the Jersey woods adjacent to the Palisades, astonished when I nearly stepped on a pheasant which shot up into a cloudless sky, trailing its improbably airborne tail feathers behind it, and where I picked what even then I must have recognized as something rare, a stalk pallid as a bone on which tiny flower bells, mottled with red and dark blue pinpricks, grew.

Despite the paucity of my early landscape, from my mother I must have acquired the love of all growing things—trees, birds, and butterflies, although mammals were not to enter my life until way past the time of my parents' prohibition. In my childhood, my early pets were toads (which I raced with paper jockeys on their backs); preying mantises, which I fed with corn worms, which they ate cob-like; turtles whose eggs hatched their tiny turtle replicas in spring; and caterpillars liquefying in their cocoons till the spring thaw gave them a new and papery birth, and blew their wings up into the exquisite lavender and dun colored wings of *cecropiae*. And to this day, when I least expect it, that moth-birthing reappears when, in the course of writing, I begin to dream.

Fifty million years ago, long before the first primates stood erect, an awkward, ungainly animal not much larger than a cat roamed Kashmir. *Indohyus* had a silhouette closely resembling that of a terrified opossum. It had a bone growth pattern characteristic of a cetacean, something not found in any other species. Its heavy outer coating and dense bones allowed it to remain submerged— much like its cousin, the modern-day hippopotamus. North Pakistan was home to *Indohyus'* cousin, *Pakicetidae.* A hoofed mammal, inhabiting an arid environment, it nonetheless drank fresh water when it could, and ate animals drinking from that water as well as some aquatic organisms living in the rivers. Its highly unusual skull identifies it as a cetacean. After a million years or so, the *Ambulocetus,* an amphibious mammal resembling a crocodile with a horse-like head, emerged. Its lower jaw housed a fat pad, like that of modern whales, allowing sound received in its lower jaw to be transmitted through its fat pad all the way to the middle ear. Its fossils are always found in shoreline marine deposits. Whales had begun returning to the sea. Primates would inherit territory. Whales made another choice.

34. Walking the Floors of the Cretaceous Sea

I don't know the desert
however often it's haunted me
In the desert absence said to me
Write!
I said: There is another writing on the mirage
It said: Write and the mirage will become green

—*from* Mahmoud Darwish: "One Traveler
Said To Another: We Won't Return"

Over 4.5 billion years the Earth has turned over in her sleep, lifted the low lands, tossed them over like blankets in her restless nights, raised the floors of the sea and pushed the dry lands beneath the deep. In a child's world, everything is possible. Windows to other worlds are without end. But for all who have eyes, who have ears, who have the sense that comes with a feeling of deep time—not the time of generations so loved by genealogists, or the sense of history favored by the patriarchs—the Earth shines her kaleidoscope.

The dream I never quite abandoned of walking on the floors of the sea became my own, way beyond the years of childhood and only because a visiting friend put my own sense of adventure to shame. We were lying in a streambed in the Yosemite high country, cooling ourselves on a scorching summer day.

"Why don't we visit the Southwest?" she asked.

I admit the idea first struck me as impossible. We were minimally equipped: a small Honda hatchback without air conditioning (this in the middle of July); a two-gallon water jug; a Coleman stove and lantern; a cooler; a pup tent; two sleeping bags; and a road map left behind by an ex-husband, eager to disappear into another marriage, a map on which, my trepidations overcome, we plotted our route, Durango at its farthest reach, near where the boundaries of four states meet. And there, many years later, where ancient seas once carved out red rock monoliths, I trod the floor of the sea as I had wanted as far back as I remembered. Sage and creosote grew where once coral fans and anemones had spread their tentacles, and in the solitary moonlight, rabbits scurried and held still where the *coelacanth* once swam when the Mississippi watershed was a lake that swathed the middle continent, dry land now where once, 145 million years ago, there was an inland sea.

In a photograph from that time I do not face the camera. I have become landscape, the landscape has become me, color of skin, color of soil, red like the red desert in the spreading rays of evening. I am an ant in a vast world of exfoliating rock, inscriptions raised there by wind and tide, etched with phantom processions of Pharaonic kings and priests, of threshers of grain and keepers of wine jars, and in the far beyond, tumbling boulders like clumsy, eyeless dwarves, put there by unseen hands to entertain the court, peopling a landscape of a scale too vast for the stunts of human clowns. Wind whispering through the sage, horses galloping in the desert wash, raising fans of water at evening—red horses, red water splashed against the setting sun, rabbits foraging under moonlight, quickening a landscape forged long before human history began, in my ears a wind breathing eternity, with us, with Earth, from the dawning of first light. In the beginning.

In the night I dreamed of a seven story mountain. No sun, no moon. Magma flowing red from the bowels of the earth. Through layers of fire furnaces belched out fiery gases. Pounding all night, hammering in the forge, the clank of industry. Fire in the furnaces belching smoke.

Day dawned, the sun shone as it always had. It was my birthing time. Forged from the place of first existence, like the poet, I emptied my mouth of silence, there in a place I knew as a garden, where all could be reborn.

35. On the Luminosity of Cells

verde que te quiero verde.	*green how i love you green.*
verde viento. verdes ramas.	*green wind. green branches.*
el barco sobre la mar	*the vessel on the sea*
y el caballo en la montaña.	*and the horse running in the mountains.*

— Federico Garcia-Lorca: *Romance sonámbulo*

Green, like the cells of my angel-wing begonia, translucent against the sunlight of morning: what looks at first like simple radiance, on closer sight reveals a scintillating world of cells, each one a separate jewel, the surfaces and undersides a play of color, green and red, mirroring the shadow colors left by absent light when its shadow haunts the retina, each cell its own transformer, each cell its own reservoir of moisture, the lips of its stomata pressed to the light.

The artful cactus hides its watery heart inside a barrel of art nouveau; the stick-plant thrives, even though it's winter outside. It shed its leaves eons ago, shrinking its surfaces to conserve moisture against the desert's scorching heat. This is Earth's conservatory where industry springs leaves and hallucinatory flowers. In the deep, if there were light and eyes to see it, watery exhibit cases would shine through their protective slime: red algae, sanguinary and delicate, furled like fallopian tubes, home to small fry, their staring eyes fixed on the zebra-striped seaworm, on sea slugs undulating in their shadowy world, knobbed as land mines, gilled like fish, their skin turquoise, ridged with gold, or colored vermilion with wine-dark lips.

Welcome to the cell museum: desert, arctic wastes, underseas guarding the secrets of their colors and their forms on Earth's whirling whirligig. Perfect beauty in their small containments, breathing, feeding, multiplying, never still. Life without cease, peopling the watery planet you call home.

36. Chasing the Miracle of Soil

Permission in my mother's house was finely measured by degrees. To turn the pages of the great art books, books picturing Persian ceramics, or tribal rugs, the only restrictions were against my own grubby hands. The Holy of Holies was her watercolor copy of a Persian miniature from the Sha Nama, Firdausi's classic poem, unfinished, and still mounted on her watercolor board, depicting the enchanted bird, the Seemurgh, returning his albino son to the Shah who had exposed him as a child to defeat the curse of his white hair, white skin, and yellow eyes. It lay carefully concealed under layers of protection in a locked drawer of what my mother called her "secretary." Search as I might, I could never find the key. I think in all the years I lived with her, she may reluctantly have allowed a peek two, or possibly three, times.

Midway between the two extremes was my mother's Botany, a small schoolgirl-sized *cahier* covered in a black fabric shellacked so that it shone like patent leather, its lines not so faint they couldn't serve as calligraphic guides. Perhaps she was as young as twelve, not older than sixteen, when some time between 1900 and 1904 she must have sat at her ink well, marking her illuminated pages with the deep blue ink, so pungent it must have wrinkled her nose, watching it dry till its surface showed coppery where it pooled, careful in all the pages never once to leave a blot. I picture her, brow furled, tip of tongue caught between clenched teeth, bent in concentration, line by line, filling her pen's tiny bladder every few minutes to even the intensity of her strokes.

Botanique

Les Cellulues
Les Bourgeons
La Fleure (here the strict calligraphy blossoms)
Le Fruit (and here it just about explodes)

In the margins of each page, tidy watercolored illustrations of cells, fruits and flowers accompany the text, treasures each one, including the glued-on edelweiss, all carefully contained at first, tight with germination, then breaking out in color, and bursting through the margins in jubilant abundance, like over-ripe fruit.

But after the sudden eruption of all that plum-y opulence, my mother gets tightlipped. A door suddenly closes. We learn nothing more about the classification of fruit than the terse listing of its four groups. Once she confessed she had a crush on her music master, Mr. Beidermann. Had he tried to kiss her blossoming cheek one day as she sat spread-hipped on the piano stool?

Permission to see her *Botanique* was rarely forthcoming. I had been "bad," or I had not been "good." Occasionally I was sick, however. Sickness was something meriting reward. At those times, tucked securely in bed, propped up on pillows, with a good reading light at my side, the *Botanique* would mysteriously appear, sprung from its hiding place. Time stilled as I turned the pages, my child's eyes buried in the cells, the leaves, the stems and branches, the cones and flowers, and last of all the fruits, the golden pears, the scarlet apples, and the deep indigo of plums dressed in frosty summer bloom. But permission granted, permission withdrawn and the notebook was slapped shut to be replaced by the dismal dinner tray and the solitary supper, downed reluctantly in bed.

37. Cosmos in the Speck of Dust

The ineffable wonder that lies hidden in the microcosm of [even] the dust particle, enclosing within the intricacies of its atomic form all the mystery of the cosmos, has also implanted in us the desire to question and understand.

—Jagadish Chandra Bose

Seeds like the ones planted in my childhood are sometimes slow to germinate. Plants taught me the miracle of soil when nearly forty years later, my mother's pages took root in my gardens—all five of them—high in the hills, and began spreading their colors under the coastal fog and the California sun.

Can a creature which has no brain as we think of it display intelligence? How can such beings manage to communicate? And is their communication indicative of an alternative intelligence at work? Plants have a *sessile habitus* or life style; that is, they are stuck in one place (a condition defined by Darwin as having their brains on the bottom, and their sex on top), and from that one place, they need to defend themselves from predators, and to obtain what they require for nourishment, growth, and reproduction. Because, compared to more mobile forms of life, they take a much slower amount of time to do all that, humans tend not to appreciate their intelligence and spectacular success. The anthropocentric view privileges brains and neurons. But plants have neither, although they do exhibit an intelligence that might be variously described as a "unifying mechanism," or a kind of "distributive intelligence," and the unique ability to survive despite the loss of up to 90 percent of their bodies. They are reported to possess between some fifteen to twenty senses, some of them analogous to ours, and a vocabulary of approximately 3,000 chemicals stored in their "libraries." Many of them produce caffeine, guaranteeing that bees will be induced to return more frequently to assist in their pollination.

In 1966, working in his laboratory late at night—so the story goes—police investigator and former CIA asset, Cleve Backster, decided to water one of his plants. On an impulse he connected one of its leaves to a polygraph machine to measure its response to water. Much to his surprise, far from becoming a better conductor, it reacted with wild excitation, just like any human undergoing a polygraph test. It occurred to him that to test this result, he would need to apply a more drastic threat. The imagery of fire entered his mind. He intended to burn the very leaf he had been testing with a match. To his amazement, the split second the image entered his mind, the polygraph tracings went haywire.

Backster hypothesized that if a plant like his *dracina* could read his mind, he should test to see if plants reacted to the death of other nearby organisms. He designed a foolproof experiment relying on his own absence from the field (to prevent any mind reading), and a random system that in his absence would dump a group of live brine shrimp into boiling water. Again, according to Backster, the reaction went "off the charts."

A recent *New Yorker* article, by Michael Pollan, reviews current thinking about the secret life of plants. Plants have little understood abilities to learn and remember the exact sound of a caterpillar chomping on the leaves of a relative (and to respond with defensive chemicals), and to locate water by sound, even though no moisture may be present, and, because they make *low clicking sounds* as their cells elongate, one scientist speculates they may actually be using these sounds as a form of echolocation. Plant experimenters have investigated how sound affects plants, and what sounds plants emit in contact with human stimulation. Cleve Backster even claimed they could pick out the individual who had injured them in a "police line-up," but many of Backster's "experiments" have not been replicable by scientists in the field.

Researchers, many of them, are focused on examining plant intelligence. They base their definitions on the plant's ability to be "on line," that is, to be aware of all the dimensions of its surroundings, and to process information, and on its abilities to problem solve. One experimenter was able to discover that, despite repeated disruptive stimuli, although they react at first, plants learn to ignore those presenting no danger to themselves. Plants also seem to possess what we might call "social intelligence;" for example, four related individual plants sharing the same pot will make room for one another and share nutrients and other resources. They show an ability to recognize kin based on the chemical signaling of their closer relatives, as opposed to more distant ones.

Plants occupy 75 percent of the Earth's surface. Ecosystem by ecosystem, they benefit from a dense web of communication. Ninety percent of them inhabit plant communities united by a web of microscopic fungi called mycorrhizae, which colonize the roots, sending extremely fine filaments that act like root extensions far out into the soil. Such fungi can sound the alarm, warning of invaders, and their filaments are more capable of nutrient and water absorption than the plant's root system itself, increasing the nutrient absorption of the plant between 100 to 1,000 times. They live in total harmony with plants, enveloping their neighbors in a great symbiotic web, and providing them (and possibly other species) communication in exchange for nourishment.

Plant behavior in the wild merits particular attention. Suzanne Simard, a forest ecologist at the University of British Columbia, described to Pollan how her colleagues "track the flow of nutrients and chemical signals through [the] invisible underground network [of the forest—which Pollan calls the 'wood-wide web']:

> They injected fir trees with radioactive carbon isotopes, then followed the spread of the isotopes through the forest community using a variety of sensing methods, including

a Geiger counter. Within a few days, stores of radioactive carbon had been routed from tree to tree. Every tree in a plot thirty meters square was connected to the network; the oldest trees functioned as hubs, some with as many as forty-seven connections. The diagram of the forest network resembled an airline route map.

The pattern of nutrient traffic showed how "mother trees" were using the network to nourish shaded seedlings, including their offspring—which the trees can apparently recognize as kin—until they're tall enough to reach the light. And, in a striking example of interspecies coöperation, Simard found that fir trees were using the fungal web to trade nutrients with paper-bark birch trees over the course of the season. The evergreen species would tide over the deciduous one when it had sugars to spare, and then call in the debt later in the season. For the forest community, the value of this coöperative underground economy appears to be better over-all health, more total photosynthesis, and greater resilience in the face of disturbance.

Research has shown that plants can monitor at least fifteen environmental variables to produce an integrated, coordinated response. For example, reacting to infrared light signals, a young plant's shoot is able to sense its nearest neighbors, and take evasive action. Some like the stilt palm will use differential growth in its roots to move away. Rhizomes, such as those of the iris, forage for richer soils, free of competitors. They will discriminate, allowing some rhizomes to begin forming leaves and flowers, while others continue to forage. Some plants like the parasitic dodder show evidence of ability to forecast future reserve allocation by assessing a prospective host by feel. If the touch is unpromising, the dodder continues its search for a host. If an individual plant or tree is attacked by pests, that individual will send out a pheromonic warning signal to its entire community and within hours, other surrounding individuals of its same species will develop chemical defenses to try to ward off similar attacks.

As early as the 19th century, scientists were measuring changes in plant conductivity in relation to external stimuli. In 1901, long before Cleve Backster submitted plants to polygraph tests, Jagadish Chandra Bose presented his findings before the British Royal Academy to skeptical response. Born in what is now Bangladesh, Bose was one of India's many polymaths, a trained physicist, biologist, botanist, archeologist and science fiction writer. His work with radio waves, anticipating Marconi, led him to understand that science could penetrate far beyond what was apparent to the naked eye. Perhaps that is what prompted him to investigate plant reactivity and plant communication. He discovered by means of instruments of his own fabrication that plants have a nervous system not unlike those of animals, and that their responses to stimuli could be measured and recorded. He discovered that an electric spasm seizes plants when they die. They are reactive to flashes of light, changes in temperature, plucking, pricking, and screaming; they grow more quickly when exposed to whispers and soothing harmonies, and poorly when exposed to unpleasantly loud noise or music. In other words, their "feelings" allow them to experience pleasure and pain.

Bose's experiments attracted the attention of prominent scientists and of George Bernard Shaw, who shuddered with horror at the convulsions of a piece of cabbage Bose once subjected to boiling water. Wrote Bose, "It was in the action of plants that I perceived the unity that was in all things...." In 1900 he demonstrated to the Royal Academy that even the responses of metals to poison and other perturbations resembled the neurological response in living organisms and that absolute barriers do not exist between the world of plants, animals, and even metals. Bose was well aware that he was bringing thousands of years of Eastern philosophy into his British-funded lab, and for a scientist living in early 20th century India who had publicly condemned the caste system, his message of the unity of all things not only had scientific and metaphysical implications, but political ones as well. It need hardly be said, the British were not impressed.

Connectedness is found in the most complex organisms, in cells in the bodies of human mothers and their children. This condition, called chimerism, was first noticed when cells containing the "Y" chromosome were found circulating in the blood of mothers after pregnancy. They could not have been the mother's own; most likely they came from the babies they carried. The phenomenon of children's cells actually living in their mother's brains might very well contribute to the extraordinarily close bond that exists between mothers and their children.

There is also evidence that cells may be transferred from mother to infant through nursing. There may be exchanges of cells between twins, and even other siblings, which may find their way back across the placenta to a younger sibling. Women may have microchimeric cells from their mothers as well as from their own children, and there even seems to be competition between cells from grandmother and infant within the mother herself. Recent findings indicate that it is common to find cells from one individual integrating into the tissues of another distinct person. Cells from other individuals are also found in the brain. Male cells were found in the brains of women and, in some cases, had been living there for several decades.

It is thought that possibly such cells may aid in tissue repair. In rats, fetal cells migrated to the maternal heart and actually differentiated into heart cells, helping to repair cell damage. In other animal studies, such cells migrated to the maternal brains and became nerve cells, possibly integrating themselves into the brain. This phenomenon may hold true for such cells in the human brain as well.

Microchimeric cells seem to aid in stimulating the immune system to arrest the growth of tumors. Many more are found in the blood of healthy women compared to those developing breast cancer, which may help to explain why childless women show a greater incidence of such tumors.

The capacity to intercommunicate on a cellular level seems to be enjoyed by the least elaborated forms of life right up along the phylogenic chain. Barbara McClintock, one of the foremost plant geneticists of all time, expressed concern that treading on grass might make it scream. When asked by colleagues how she could manage to see under the microscope what had eluded other researchers, she replied she just had a "feeling for the organism." Whenever she focused on a cell under the microscope, she "just got in there, and had a look around" because through her work she had come to recognize the connectedness of things.

Ever since 1859 when Darwin first proposed his tree-of-life interpretation of evolution, perhaps because it placed *homo sapiens sapiens* at the summit of living organisms, scientists and most of the public (except the 31 percent of U.S. citizens who, as of 2014, believe that God created humans 6,000 to 10,000 years ago) have been quite willing to accept his explanations with very little fuss. But already in 1905 alternative ideas were stirring, notably with the work of Konstantin Mereshkovsky, a Russian biologist, whose lichen research (like Beatrice Potter's of *Peter Rabbit* fame) led him to advance the theory of symbiogenesis, namely that complex cells had evolved from earlier symbiotic relationships between simple ones. The late biologist, Lynn Margulis, built on such theories, and in a series of experiments, papers and books published over a long and distinguished career proposed the fundamental idea that life itself first evolved from prokaryotes, simple cells lacking a nucleus, and that the origin of more complex cells, the eukaryotes, came about with the invasion by prokaryotes of other prokaryotes, so that over time, the invader became the nucleus of the host cell. This quantum leap distinguishes the single-celled prokaryotes from the nucleus-bearing eukaryotes—an *even greater* distinction than that existing between plant and animal cells. Whereas Darwin's model proposes a vertical evolution, suggesting *hierarchy* from lower to higher forms based on procreative competition, Margulis proposes a latticework of *collaborative* interpenetrations between cells so primitive they lacked nuclei:

> The...total discontinuity between living forms with and without nuclei...suggests that the new cells were begotten by a process fundamentally different from simple mutation or bacterial genetic transfer. The scientific work of the past decade has convinced us that this process was symbiosis. Independent prokaryotes entered others. With time these

populations of coevolved bacteria became communities of microbes so deeply interdependent, they were, for all practical purposes, single stable organisms—protists.... Under certain pressures [they] behaved as single wholes. Individual bacteria bec[a]me the organelles of nucleated cells; nucleated cells team[ed] up into many-celled 'individuals' trillions of times their size.

The science of endosymbiosis proposes that life on Earth originated, not only with competitive natural selection but with *collaborative* relationships between cells of different individuals, ultimately resulting in the co-existence in our own human bodies of about three pounds of bacteria, which allow us to digest and perform all the other bodily functions without which none of us can live. *By implication, this discovery at the very root of existence might be seen as suggesting a collaborative worldview in rich contradistinction to that of the West.*

Microcosmos, one of many books Margulis co-wrote with her son, Dorion Sagan, concludes with a description of the work of James Lovelock, the atmospheric chemist who devised the Gaia hypothesis. While working at NASA on ways to detect life on Mars, Lovelock found that gases which would normally react quickly and completely to make stable compounds somehow co-exist in Earth's atmosphere where they remain aloof, that is, they somehow avoid reacting, apparently bypassing the laws of standard equilibrium chemistry. Considering the quantity of oxygen in Earth's atmosphere, methane, nitrogen, carbon monoxide, and nitrous oxide should be found only in minute quantities, and yet they are millions and in one case trillions of times more abundant than normal, as explained by chemistry alone.

The only way Lovelock could explain such a remarkable phenomenon was to attribute it to the collective action of living microorganisms continually producing renewed amounts of these reactive gases.

Probably everyone has experienced the phenomenon of the overheated lecture hall, or concert auditorium. At the start of the event, the temperature is usually at such a comfortable level, people are hardly conscious of it, but at the end of two hours or so, the heat of so many bodies breathing in a closed space has raised the temperature to uncomfortable levels. So with Earth, whose atmosphere functions, as does that of a room, as a closed system, but with air-conditioned properties.

Judging from fossil evidence, from the beginning of life on Earth, living biota have been regulating, not only the composition of gases on a global scale, but Earth's temperature as well. Applying this hypothesis to the planet Mars, Lovelock's spectroscopes detected a chemistry whose balance was entirely predictable on the basis of physics and chemistry *alone.* Therefore, he reasoned, life must be absent on Mars. When the space probe landed in 1976, the on-board experiments showed definitively that life did not exist on Mars. (The cost of the experiment: U.S. $1 billion in 1976 dollars, $1 billion, which might better have been applied to the study and prevention of global warming and eventual collapse of the very atmosphere Lovelock was studying.) Here is Lovelock:

> Life first appeared on Earth about 3,500,000…years ago. From that time until now, the presence of fossils shows that the Earth's climate has changed very little. Yet the output of heat from the sun, the surface properties of the Earth, and the composition of the atmosphere have almost certainly varied greatly over the same period.

Lovelock's conclusion: living organisms, through their effect on water and on water-bearing clouds modulate Earth's systems in an on-going feedback loop. The question, *Is there intelligent life?* applies, if not necessarily to the human species, most assuredly to the most humble, least complex of organisms—the bacteria— attesting to the unity of all things, from the very smallest to the macrocosm itself.

But, by the same token, Lovelock cautions that,

> Gaian responses to changes for the worse must obey the rules of cybernetics, where the time constant and the loop gain are important factors. Thus [atmospheric] regulation

has a time constant measured in thousands of years. Such slow processes give the least warning of undesirable trends. By the time it is realized that all is not well and action is [finally] taken, inertial drag will bring things to a worse state before an equally slow improvement can set in.

The ultimate meaning underlying these discoveries is two-fold: If the use of fossil fuels were to cease today, like the temperature in the concert hall, their hothouse effect would continue to increase for the next 200 years; and that indeed, *all life is interconnected,* as mystics and so-called "primitive" people have tried to tell us from the very beginning.

In this apparently progressive civilization, so progressive it relies exclusively on scientific validation, here is where the science of life and intuitive awareness finally join hands. But are the planet's contemporary social and economic arrangements reflective of that understanding? Climate deniers take notice: the flood you drown in may be of your own making.

VI.

OUTLIVING CIVILIZATION

38. Confessions of a Speciesist

Will leviathan make supplication unto thee? Wilt thou make him a covenant? or wilt thou indenture him forever?
—Job 4: 3-4

Some months ago as I sat unsuspecting in a darkened movie house, watching "Chasing Ice," observing images of vast glaciers—some bigger than Manhattan—melt and rush headlong into the sea, a whale crept up on me and cunningly addressed me.

"What has your species done to the seas around us?"

You asked for no explanation, you required no excuse.

"Tell me," you said, "how you justify what your species has done to the Earth."

A year of delay and obfuscation has gone by and still I have not answered your question. Coming from you, I may have given your question less weight. Or I went about it roundabout. I visited the world of other mammals: elephants, wolves, and beings like yourself. I visited the first men and the young and the poets of my species. I found that other living beings also have ways of speaking, often with clicking sounds—even plants, even stones—and that, on those grounds alone, my species, whose first language was punctuated with clicking sounds, is no more unique than plants, or molds, or bacteria, or pebbles in the sea. I came to understand that now in the light of actual proof that all life forms, plant, animal, and even mineral are connected, the hierarchical arrangements characterizing human life are deeply flawed, and fundamentally unscientific; and although when it suits us, we pretend to worship science and technology as our new religion, we are living sacrilegiously in an unholy world of our own making.

I went back deep in time to seek some explanation. I fastened my attention on the West because of its history of conquest, colonization, globalization and the unbridled arrogance and destruction it has visited on our planet, but in the process, quite unaware, I discovered I had became a speciesist, like all those of my kind who assured me from the Age of the Patriarchs: "Thou shalt have dominion over all the Earth."

Until now I have not answered you directly. Nor can I master your language in all its complexity, with its clicks and hums and whistles. But all the while I dragged my feet, you were asking musically, and in rhymed verse:

"DUDE, WHAT HAVE YOU DONE TO MY PLANET?"

And all the while I prevaricated, the glaciers went on melting. All the time I delayed, TEPCO continued hemorrhaging billions of gallons of radioactive water into the Pacific. During the year gone past, Fukushima's radioactive plume continued to make its slow, inexorable crawl toward the vast continent far to the east. And all the while I marked time, 87 percent of the world's over 400 nuclear reactors continued to operate, piling up 330,000 tons of nuclear waste with no technology in sight to guarantee safe storage for the next 4.5 billion years—the half life of U_{238} —it will require to keep it sequestered from the Earth's biosphere.

Over the year I delayed, Earth's one billion cars continued to dump six billion tons of carbon dioxide into the atmosphere; coal plants continued to burn, mountains were shaved to extract more, the integrity of the ground was fractured in an insane scramble for more natural gas, belching more fossil fuels at a time when the atmosphere teeters on the breaking point of 400 parts per million; planes, merchant and cruise ships plying the seas continued to foul the air, and the melting polar cap feedback loop sped up its release of methane from two meter-wide breaks in the sea ice, to gaps more than one kilometer wide. The seas became acidified and carbon-saturated to a level at which they can absorb little more. Fracking companies injected more than 780 million gallons of hydraulic fracturing products, many of them toxic and carcinogenic into the ground, permanently contaminating the aquifers. West Coast marine die-offs, collapsing scallop, starfish and jellyfish populations littered the seafloor.

On January 8, 2014, severely undersize, conjoined gray whale twins were born whose bodies washed up in the Mexican Ojo de Liebre lagoon, a phenomenon never seen before.

Another forest, the size of New Jersey, was cut down to make room for more grazing and crop cultivation and more housing developments. Geo-engineers poured more iron into the seas, and more aluminum salts into the ionosphere, manipulating the earth's atmosphere; plant microbiologists designed hybrid seeds to remove their naturally regenerating (but not their crop contaminating) power; pesticide use continued to decimate bee populations so that in some areas of the world humans are now forced to pollinate fruit trees by hand; and half the world's wealth has been poured into the coffers of war and war-making, killing millions, and contaminating the soils, water and air wherever marauding armies bivouac. One hundred fifty million more humans have been born to help lay waste the Earth's remaining resources. Citizens of Beijing flock to giant TV screens to watch a virtual sunrise because for some time now, sunrise and sunset have been blocked from view by a miasma of polluted air. And this year's drought will force next year's humans to choose between eating and driving when crops begin to fail and famine stalks the Earth. From Maine to Florida, humans won't have to decide whether land sink or sea rise carried their houses out to sea. Climate collapse will have decided for them.

As an issue, the Earth's population is the elephant-in-the-room, one that remains top secret, "classified." The Population Connection seems to be one of few organizations determined to address it. But all is not lost—not yet. America's finest news source* reports that an International Panel on Climate has fundamentally reshaped our understanding of climate collapse. Lead author, John Bartlett, is quoted as saying, "Our research...proved conclusively that, year after year, the acceleration of global warming and the [man-made] damage [it] cause[s] can be linked to *7 billion main culprits....* Consequences of climate change were widely known [for decades] yet these specific individuals did nothing to curb...their practices. Now that we have identified the key players responsible, we can...[hold] them accountable.

IPCC officials confirmed that, since the report was released this morning, 153,007 more [newborn culprits] have been added to the list of top contributors to global warming."*

39. A Short but Sobering Biographical Note

Sometime before my mother reached adolescence, my grandfather invented the first electrically powered automobile in Switzerland. Although he also held a patent for an air cooler, his collaborator-engineer sold it to the Ford Motor Company, which had swapped electrically powered engines for gasoline-driven ones as early as 1896. My grandfather's electric roadster was a narrow, open little cracker box that rode high above its nervy little wheels. Every Sunday four people could perch up there in high style and circle Lake Neuchatel at a glorious 15 miles an hour (1.6 times speedier if they drove in kilometers).

Besides my grandfather, that left room for my grandmother (for whom I am named, and who shares a birthday exactly 100 years to the day with my elder son) and my mother's two brothers, Paul and Marcel (the hellion of the family, whose peaked left eyebrow I inherited—but not his disposition). That left my mother and her two sisters out—which is perhaps why she got the patriarchal message and left home at 18, but not why her two sisters died in childhood of diphtheria. Although I grew up never knowing what a family car might feel like, I can forgive her life-long devotion to the motorcar. *"Quel magnifique automobile!"* she exclaimed every time she saw a shiny American vehicle splashing its way through New York City's slushy streets.

My grandfather loved to dream up new inventions, which he liked to do on fishing expeditions. He'd reel in on a pier somewhere, moving backwards all the time—still dreaming—and sometimes he fell in. The man enjoyed great powers of concentration, which is good for an inventor, but less than ideal on fishing trips.

---

* *The Onion,* January 21, 2014

My grandfather's devotion to the bicycle as a means of transportation was at best lukewarm, which is why, although he sported a no-nonsense handlebar moustache, and waxed it morning and night, he always went to bed with his motoring cap on. His average fishing catch was 10 kilograms (even more in pounds) because there were more fish to catch in those pollution-free, pre-global warming days, but he may not have given too much thought to the consequence of his invention.

According to Jan Lundberg, interviewed in 2007, in the United States each year automobiles kill 46,000 people, and asphyxiate 30,000 more who die of respiratory illnesses. Automobile fuel releases 17 percent of all carbon dioxide emissions, almost but not quite equal to rainforest destruction. Exhaust causes $2 to $4 billion in damages to food crops, not including other costs of air pollution, which brings the total to an impressive $200 billion. One million animals, large and small, become road kill every day.

In America, nearly half the urban area is devoted to cars, more space than gets allocated to housing, however not the main explanation for why there are so many homeless, except for the 100,000 people displaced every year by highway construction. American pavement now covers over 60,000 square miles, roughly the area of North Dakota; the black of asphalt retains the sun's heat and helps keep the planet nice and toasty, more with each passing year. To maintain existing roads the U.S. would have to spend $25 billion a year, yet it penny pinches only $13 billion, but pops a cool $200 million a day (that's $73 billion a year) building new ones to make sure that it can't possibly maintain them farther down the line.

In the 30 years from 1960 to 1990 the number of licensed drivers nearly doubled; the percentage of folks who drove to work increased from 70 to 87 percent, those commuting by public transit decreased 50 percent, folks walking to work dropped from 10 to 4 percent, and the number of kids walking or biking to school dropped from 60 to 10 percent, thanks to all those soccer moms.

Congestion increased from 40 to 70 percent, reducing average city speeds to under six miles an hour, which makes walking just as efficient and much more effective against obesity. It is responsible for increasing fuel waste by 7 million gallons a year, costing drivers a cool additional $41 billion—and adding another 73 million tons of CO_2 to the atmosphere. If you divide travel distance per year by the time you spend pampering your vehicle (with paper work and simonizing), your speed comes down to five miles an hour (faster in kilometers of course).

While cars choke the roads, NGOs (who mostly fly, and drive to work) raise the cry: *Save The Earth! Save The Wolves! Save The Polar Bears!* What's wrong with starting at the bottom first? SAVE THE EARTHWORMS! SAVE THE KRILL FOR GOD SAKES! SAVE THE PLANKTON! SAVE THE BACTERIA! SAVE THE FUNGI! SAVE THE DAD-BLAMED NEMATODES! That's what's at the bottom of the food chain, *for crying out loud!* Without these Kings of Dirt, we don't eat. But does anyone push any of these campaigns? Has anyone ever heard of them? No! They're not sexy! Bacteria aren't cuddly. All folks can think of is their precious little feely, fury mammals— the ones that look the most like them. There's a reason no one ever tries to save the chickens or the pigs. And you can bet when folks discover the finger-licking taste of roast wolf and polar bear, it's curtains for them, too.

But most of the air pollution caused by car use doesn't spew from the tailpipe (fooled you there!)—it comes from the metals mining and manufacturing processes required before these dragons of the new religion even hit the roads. But it will take more than an archangel disguised as Bill McKibben to administer the *coup de grace.*

40. Making Peace With Reality

In a 2014 article titled "Militarism and Violence are So Yesterday: It's Time to Make Peace the Reality," Kevin Zeese and Margaret Flowers make the case that the time has come to embrace nonviolent practices. In particular, they emphasize that the United States, which spends more then $1 trillion each year on its war pathology—more than all the militaries of the world combined—while its infrastructure crumbles, the planet continues to warm, and human needs go unmet, can no longer support its imperial aspirations; that its high-fallutin' posture is killing not only other nations but itself as well, while making mince meat of the planet. They cite the report by Project Censored that calls the U.S. Department of Defense—including private military contractors and the weapons industry—the worst polluters on the planet. And now with the so-called Pacific Pivot's show of strength, the United States is surrounding Asia—from de-stabilizing Ukraine to building yet another base on Jeju Island, a world heritage site—with all the grace of a subway exhibitionist.

The late Rosalie Bertell, the fearless nun mathematician and physicist, who followed her seminal work on nuclear energy, *No Immediate Danger* (1985), with *Planet Earth* (2001) points out the ways in which U.S. violence is killing the Earth and bleeding all of its people, especially those in the Third World. Zeroing in on the first Gulf War, she claims the U.S. made a profit of $53 billion, while it cost forty low and middle-income countries one percent of their GDP. The cost to Yemen was 10 percent of its GDP, and to Jordan a monster 25 percent. Although the UN charter provides for compensation to members affected by Security Council decisions, and although it reported a net income at the time, the World Bank failed to provide compensation to any of the 40 African countries most affected by the war.

Although in 2001 some 33 percent of the world's children were living in poverty, by refusing to sign the Declaration of the Rights of the Child the U.S. still retains the option of executing children who commit violent crimes, and imprisoning them with adults, including 15-year-old Omar Khadr, whom it held for ten years in Guantanamo until, as an adult, he was repatriated to Canada where he remained in prison for another 20 months before a Canadian judge refused to block his release. At the world summit on the Rights of the Child, it was estimated that preserving the health and safety of the world's children would require a minimum yearly outlay of $25 billion to provide safe drinking water and sanitation, family planning education and reduction of maternal and child deaths, literacy programs, supplementary food programs, and community health, yet the 2001 Pentagon funding request for the U.S. Missile Defense Project alone was $30.2 billion.

A recent article published in *Global Research*, by Rick Rozoff, drew a parallel between the March aggressions of Nazi Germany preceding World War II and the pattern of the United States: March 1999 saw the start of the U.S.-NATO "Operation Allied Force," fought over seventy-eight days against the federal Republic of Yugoslavia. More "operations" were to follow. In March, 2003, "Iraqi Freedom" [to despoil] involved troops of its NATO surrogate collaborating with the U.S. in the invasion and occupation (and destruction) of Iraq. In March 2011, with "Operation Odyssey Dawn," the U.S. launched a more than six-month-long air war and naval blockade against Libya. One shudders to contemplate that the pattern of March aggressions may go as far back as the Kurgan invasion of Europe.

Since 1999, in all, a total of ten states have been "seriously, more than likely fatally, wounded or destroyed," either through direct, or covert, or proxy wars staged by the U.S. and NATO: the Federal Republic of Yugoslavia (splintered into three states); Afghanistan, Iraq, Somalia, Ivory Coast, Libya, Yemen, Syria, Sudan, and Mali (see http://www.globalresearch.ca/ukraine-syria-venezuela-and-beyond-beware-the-wars-of-march/5373639). According to Michel Chossudovsky, writing in *Global Research*, the pattern of U.S. gold confiscation in Iraq and Libya, known as "operation airlift," seems to have been repeated in the Ukraine in 2014 where, according to *Iskra*, on March 7, an unmarked transport loaded up Ukraine's gold reserves and whisked them off to the United States. And, it is now confirmed, the U.S. congress has voted overwhelmingly to send weapons to the Ukraine, which clearly represents an act of war—war against nuclear-powered Russia.

Contrary to promotional claims, military activities reduce available jobs. As early as 1990-92, Bertell claimed that if the UK had cut its 1990-2 military budget in half, it would have actually created 520,000 more jobs and increased its GDP by nearly two percent. Although UK military producers made $3,267,000 in profit in those years, they also reduced the number of jobs by 89,869. She capped her discussion with U.S. Bureau of Labor Statistics: one billion dollars could have produced 76,000 military related jobs, in contrast to 187,000 in education—more than twice as many. More recent statistics published by the U.S. Bureau of Labor suggest that one billion dollars would procure 187,000 jobs in education, or 139,000 in the health sector, or 100,000 construction jobs, or 92,000 transportation jobs *in contrast to only* 76,000 jobs in the military.

Above all, Bertel stressed that each military conflict continues to degrade the Earth's resources, including its arable land. In 2001, worldwide available land to support life totaled about five acres per capita with no provision made to set aside any land for preserving biodiversity, yet since WWII, one-sixth of the world's vegetated regions has been degraded, and 25 percent of that degradation has been from causes other than farming.

By its own statistics, NATO has caused environmental degradation with leaks of toxic substances during military transport, atmospheric pollution of coastal areas, air and water pollution from ship engines, transportation of contaminating materials along water ways, dumping of radioactive waste, noise pollution, and chemical accidents. Bertell makes the obvious point that like corporations, the military—although somewhat clumsy at winning wars—is adroit at externalizing its costs to the environment, while helping itself to natural resources. In general, the standard corporate practice of socializing costs and privatizing gains speaks to the unsustainability of the world's present economic arrangements. The professional journal *Nature* puts the present global costs of such "free" services at $33 trillion per year.

The shift occurring over the past twenty-five years in the world's political systems, characterized by globalization and austerity programs, clearly signals abandonment of the basic principles of democracy. And without its restoration, there is no way that our steepeningly disparate hierarchical systems can ever be repaired. There is no going back by working within moribund systems to redeem a bad design. In the U.S., for example, taxing marijuana—the trade-off for "legalizing" it—will empty the prisons of cheap plantation labor, while intensifying structural unemployment that, were it to be honestly reported, would hover now around 20 percent because those corporations exploiting that labor (including the government itself) will simply offshore their labor requirements to whichever country offers the lowest going rate. The same holds true for overturning Citizens United, which would do nothing to deprive elected officials of their exploding campaign war chests, reserves which they would simply feel the need to stoke by other means. Raising taxes on financial transactions, in principle designed to balance an uncontrolled budget, would fuel increased military expenditure and do nothing to reverse the course of fascism (or to alleviate student loan indebtedness) as long as a Valkyrie government is hell-bent on riding off to ever-proliferating wars.

Principles are needed before priorities can be set, but they will never come from profit-driven elites. For the past many years, not only the financial industry but also the "defense" industries have systematically eroded the personal assets of the great majority of the Earth's people. War and global warming have done the rest. But in the end the beginning may emerge: in *Blessed Unrest*, Paul Hawken documents the millions of organizations which now exist offering alternative ways of reimagining the world. Yet in order to re-democratize our political lives, analysis is required to identify where capitalism's supports can best be cut off at the knees.

The website of the World People's Conference on Climate Change and the Rights of Mother Earth, held in Bolivia in 2010, attests to the dedicated deliberations by seventeen working groups to develop analyses, position papers, and action plans to confront the global warming that results from the enslavement of peoples and nature by the mechanisms of commercial profit. A statement by working group 1, "Structural Causes," lays responsibility firmly where it belongs: "We are faced with a profound structural crisis as a consequence of having reached the planet's limits. We are confronted with the terminal crisis of a patriarchal development model based in the slavery and destruction of human beings and nature."

The "Law of Mother Earth," first promulgated by Bolivia on October 15, 2011, the same year as Fukushima, enshrines the rights of Earth, and institutionalizes veneration of the Andean deity, Pachamama, by establishing a bill of rights for Earth. It was structured in such a way as to effect the fundamental ecological reorientation of Bolivian society and economy, requiring that all existing and future laws adapt to it and accept the ecological limits set by nature. (At a recent Tribunal in Defense of the Rights of Mother Earth, held in Oakland, California, indigenous speakers pointed out that the word "nature" evokes a concept of separation originating with the Enlightenment, and that a more language-appropriate term, Earth, affirms connection between all living beings.) It calls for a public policy guided by *sumaj kawsay*—an indigenous concept translated as "living well," or living in harmony with nature and people—in place of current imperatives to produce more goods and stimulate consumption. The rights of Mother Earth so defined are seven: the right to life, to its diversity, to water, to clean air, to Earth's restoration, to re-establishing Earth's equilibrium, and to life free of contamination; but it has been unable to slow, let alone deter, Bolivia's extractive economy, which depends on mining and on building new roads into outlying areas of the country in anticipation of continued "development."

Recent Bolivian history marks the trajectory leading up to the law's development. Now actually forming part of the constitution not only of Bolivia but of Ecuador as well, it reflects the influence of the Global Peoples' Conference On Climate Change held in Cochabamba in April of 2010, which pulled together peoples and communities to research and develop concrete alternatives to dominant systems of exploitation.

Ten years before, the city of Cochabamba had been rocked by a people's revolt. Bechtel Corporation, in a consortium with other entities and overseen by the World Bank, attempted to privatize its water rights, cutting off both potable and irrigation water, and prohibiting taking water directly from sources such as lagoons, rivers, or springs as people had done for centuries. Water rates increased 300 percent, cutting off the water supply to the poorest people (a foreshadowing of what is now occurring in Detroit). The revolt, led by trade unionist Oscar Olivera, ousted Bechtel, much to the consternation of the World Bank.

In the intervening years, Olivera has visited many communities in various countries, from Chiapas in Mexico to communities in France, to learn how people organize and govern themselves. He believes change to halt the power of capitalism can only come about through collective action outside of political parties or governments. Says Olivera: "I believe that these alternative forms must network with one another, and…form the basis for a new world. We have no other choice."

Olivera feels that the human right to water is a fundamentally Western concept because water is a necessity not only for people but for mountains and for animals and for the Earth as a living being. Speaking of Evo Morales, president of Bolivia, Olivera thinks that although he plays well in the international arena, he doesn't much care for the real interests and problems of the people. Olivera repeatedly refused Morales' invitations to accept the formal government position of Minister of Water. Says Olivera, "I always declined, because I did not see in Morales the readiness to dismantle a state apparatus, which turned everyone who worked in it into a thief and a liar and which did not work for the people. I said to Morales that I would not change like those who ended up in the government. The state apparatus must be taken apart, opened to the people and the power given to the people."

Confirming Olivera's view, on October 7, 2014, Evo Morales announced plans by the Bolivian government to invest $2 million to develop Bolivia's first nuclear plant, scheduled to go on line in 2025 in the province of La Paz.

Initiatives like the 2010 conference and the writing of the Constitution of the Rights of Mother Earth, trumpet as they may, reflect only the very first glimmerings of a movement that needs to capture the global imagination if it is to result in actual structural change. Despite such devotion to reimagining a harmonious world, four years later it has become clear that the only quantifiable change that has occurred is in the area of public discussions such as this and subsequent ones, which serve the vital function of building global awareness that another world is possible, but at the same time, it confirms that change cannot come about through the UN, through climate conferences, or for that matter in any top/down institutionalized framework, and that, on the contrary, it must take place at the grassroots level, much as the collective Earthbody builds an autoimmune system, cell by cell, to rid itself of disease.

At the local level, Thomas Linzey, whose background is in the area of public interest law, works to help people in rural U.S. communities who, as they write in constitutional rights for local ecosystems, at the same time write in the rights of Earth as well. Through a process of trial and error, Linzey has developed an alternative approach to lawyering, but by his own admission, he has been slow to fully apprehend how the present legal system cannot "work." Through CELDF, his organization based in Philadelphia, Linzey's first appeals, representing people determined to bar waste incinerators, hog farming, toxic sludge, and later fracking from their communities, were directed at the DEP, Pennsylvania's regulatory agency. He based his defense on the grounds that the corporations involved had failed to file permit applications correctly, thus obtaining ninety-day stays—just long enough for the corporation to return with an updated application. The DEP automatically licensed their right to locate because the laws applicable to environmental regulation are written in collaboration with the very corporations they are designed to regulate.

"Keep in mind that the verb 'to regulate' postulates that what is regulated has [already] been allowed," Linzey points out. Complicating matters mightily is the section of the 14th Amendment Civil Rights Act of 1866, originally intended to protect the voting rights of former slaves which, ever since 1871, has been claimed by corporations to legitimize their status as persons, and, as such, permits them to initiate lawsuits against other parties for damages and loss of profits.

Because the structure of the law didn't allow even a community majority to use the courts to insure the kind of community it wanted, the CELDF staff was prompted to come up with a new, more proactive strategy. They formed the Pennsylvania Family Farm coalition, a coalition which included family farmers, four hundred municipal government representatives; the Sierra Club and other environmental groups; organized labor as well as the Pennsylvania Association For Sustainable Agriculture; and the Pennsylvania Farmers Union. For a time the coalition was able to defeat legislation designed to stop elected rural municipal officials' attempts to ban agribusiness and toxic sludge from their communities. But their victory was short lived when a new piece of legislation passed through the state legislature to be signed into law by Pennsylvania's Democratic governor.

As a result, farmers were prompted to engage in an informal process of self-education, which confirmed their understanding that under the inalienable civil and political rights guaranteed by the Constitution, they had the right to determine the course of their own communities. From that effort came the request by a rural Pennsylvania township that Linzey draft an ordinance to deprive corporations of exercising their constitutional rights in their municipality. Responding to that request, CELDF drafted the Corporate Rights Elimination Ordinance. Township by township, Pennsylvania rural municipalities passed binding ordinances refusing to acknowledge constitutional rights for corporations in their townships.

Linzey cites the growing feeling that there needs to be a new framework of governance in the United States. People are studying the Constitution as the organ of property and commerce, and challenging its appropriateness on two grounds: drafted by the founding fathers, it effectively represented the interests of only 20 percent of the population, that of propertied white men, to the exclusion of women, slaves, indentured servants, people of color (First Nations and blacks), and white men without property. As an 18th century document and product of the Enlightenment, it cannot adequately address global problems such as those which exist all too emergently today.

Already municipalities in forty-three states have written "home rule" laws, allowing citizens to dismantle old municipal governments and erect new ones to replace them. Home rule separates their communities from governance by the state, allowing them to do everything not prohibited by the Constitution. As such, home rule effectively overrides the limited effectiveness of purely environmental ordinances.

Following this development, it became apparent to Linzey that rather than defining sustainable communities by default, a new vehicle was needed to enable communities to proactively design a new vision that defines who they are. Instead of adhering to the constraints of the commerce-and-property Constitution that now exists, a re-envisioned Constitution providing for the rights of nature is needed that would allow communities to write in constitutional rights for ecosystems, while depriving corporations of constitutional rights.

With the spread of this kind of local legislation throughout rural Pennsylvania, people in other states began to clamor for legal remedies of their own. But the new kind of home-rule ordinance is not the "product," as Linzey explains, so much as people working together to de-colonize their thinking in order better to grasp that at issue is the structure of U.S. governance that deprives them of their rights at the local level, and that this structure needs to be replaced in a fundamental way.

To handle expanding national interests, CELDF was prompted to institute an educational program which it named after a toxic pollution victim: the Daniel Pennock Democracy Schools. Their educational efforts have allowed people to gain a better understanding of the rights of people vs. those of corporations, and to learn how to reframe their single issues in ways effective enough to take on basic power structures. Already there are fifteen permanent school locations throughout the U.S. and now the organization is slowly extending the effort to other countries.

Speaking more recently, in October 2014, in the Yukon, Mari Margil, a CELDF associate, reported how moving forward, the organization is working to help communities "constitutional-ize" protection for human, community and Earth rights, a movement which has the potential eventually of moving from the local into the state level. But she emphasizes that change needs to start locally, and not to imagine that somehow it can successfully be grafted onto a structurally dysfunctional system.

Meanwhile, mindful practice and single-issue activism, while helpful on both public and private levels, may in fact slow the re-democratization of our world by keeping people fragmented and oblivious to the need of forming wider coalitions if we are to defeat the neo-con agenda. Some of these may include: powering down, in terms of life-style changes such as making do with less; participating in the sharing economy; walking more and driving less; direct barter for goods and services; energy conservation; and shifting energy sources away from fossil fuel consumption to use of renewables. Others may include reimagining education to reflect collaborative as opposed to hierarchical values; promoting critical thinking vs. testing to the core curriculum; and de-commodifying art to support alternative, experimental forms of theater, dance, music, publication, as well as visual forms.

Other initiatives may include:

- Demilitarization of U.S. society
- Opposition to atomic weapons, the use of drones, chemical and biological warfare
- Counter-recruitment
- Stopping King C.O.N.G. (Coal, Oil, Nukes, & Natural Gas)
- Developing a People's Energy Program

Moving communities towards a happiness economy includes among others:

- Local, technologically appropriate farming
- Prison reform
- Establishing worker-owned businesses and cooperatives
- Establishing state and postal banks
- Fostering community democracy projects which place municipal budgets under popular control
- Establishing community land trusts
- Local principle reduction

Every one of the initiatives briefly listed above represents conscious efforts based on economic analysis and on more appropriate responses to human needs, but they are surface palliatives at best, band aids applied in the larger context of a fundamentally dysfunctional system. Change, if it is to become truly structural, can only take place outside entrenched systems. At the same time, such single-issue changes must be driven by a broader recognition that the over-arching issue uniting every separate single issue has to be the *affirmation of democracy* in a political landscape—with no space left for democratic praxis.

Even more critical is the need to free ourselves from the unconsciously assimilated constraints imposed on us by the languages we speak, languages which have imprinted our collective psyche and which our speaking (and later writing) has reinforced daily by use and reuse, for over 6,500 years, from the beginnings of the Kurgan invasion where our languages originate. How will this be done? An instructive approach might be to learn from the constraints found in many of the languages of the Americas, which disallow fundamental assumptions held dear by the West, which privilege the individual to the detriment of the commonwealth. A list of concepts in need of re-examination, limited as it is, suggests ways to begin encountering the deeply held worldview perpetuated by the linguistic constraints of the West. Some of the more obvious might include:

Re-Defining 'Us;' Decapitalizing 'I'

The primary task of the West, if we are to overcome the deeply embedded assumptions of our very languages, is to re-define the 'Us,' abandoning the cult of the individual in favor of a world view that legitimizes and indeed prioritizes the collective. Aside from asset disparity now affecting 99 percent of the U.S. population, there is the matter of what happens beyond our national borders. Most of us see no connection between our own lives of relative plenty and the lives of those living in dearth. We seem to be unconcerned with their suffering, whether it be domestic or foreign. We pass the homeless in the streets without so much as a look. We fail to recognize how poverty relates to our own overconsumption. Most of us still don't see the killing on December 12, 2013, of fifteen Yemeni wedding guests by a U.S. drone strike as any of our business. (See http://www.hrw.org/node/123244/section/3).

Until this indifference is amended, Americans themselves are destined to become the unfortunate victims of economic dearth and of drone use *domestically,* through corporate greed and by a "government" out to "protect" us, and there won't be anything to be done about it *because* enough of us are not yet paying appropriate attention when it happens to others. If nothing else, there's nothing wrong with practicing a bit of rhetorical reversal. How would we feel, for example, if something more bloody than bloody marys were to be served at our own wedding receptions? How would we feel if we were invaded and occupied by another country? Would we break out the champagne and roses?

What is our responsibility to the great whales, and to all other living beings with whom we fail to share the planet? Which leads to:

Re-Defining Our Relationship to Property

Attitudes to ownership need to shift. It is interesting to note that in some of their first encounters with First Nations people, Europeans accused them of theft. But many First Nations people's use of resources was shared. If one household experienced need, its members did not hesitate to help themselves from other households to obtain what they required. The basic assumption here has to do with the agent to whom ownership is attributed: for the West it stays with the individual or the immediate circle, whether public or private; a contrasting attitude attributes ownership to all mankind, ultimately deriving from the Great Mother Herself, which ultimately implies re-sacralizing the Earth herself.

Re-Defining Territory

Related to ownership is the concept of territory. Because humankind inhabits land, it is forced to be governed by its limitability, its relative ability to support life, and its very gravity. Some First Nations and marine animal life offer useful models in contrast to the concept of territoriality, namely what we have earlier referred to as agreements, or arrangements. Animals have learned to keep out of one another's way. Some First Nations people managed to live (before contact) by obeying similar imperatives. Irreconcilable differences were settled by migration to new territory, or by dividing tribes into clans. Such solutions worked then because more space was available, and populations were controlled by infant mortality and high death rates.

Acknowledging that human history has moved beyond the pre-historic, it becomes clear that, although certain natural forces still act to limit human population growth, human fertility far outstrips them. Animals such as the wolf, and human tribes such as the Ju/wasi, offer useful models as to how fertility might be controlled. The alternatives are either "family planning" (the euphemism for fertility control) or infanticide. In our own society, the mention of infanticide may strike a jarring note, but in its obsessions—on the one hand, with restricting the availability of birth control and abortion; on the other, its cynical indifference to the nurture of new life—the United States, ranking 46th in infant mortality statistics, the lowest of any industrial country in the world, might very well be viewed as practicing slow infanticide by poor nutrition, unavailable maternal and neonatal care, and virtually non-existent maternity leave. It might be accused of practicing the even slower infanticide of barely raising each new crop of newborns to the point where it reaches enlistment age, which leads to:

Re-Defining the Where

Replacing a national boundary concept based on the understanding that national boundaries, set along territorial lines, most of them arbitrary, cannot stabilize such ephemeral and changing elements as ethnic populations and their migrations, air and wind movements, influence of tides and current, as well as the contamination by potentially Earth-destroying technologies, such as nuclear plants, whose potential for catastrophe is impervious to national containment given wind and water patterns. Replacing them with concepts based on planetary limitations including ability to absorb CO_2 emissions, methane releases, and contaminating plumes, which leads to:

Replacing Concepts of Unlimited Growth

Given that, despite the exquisitely balanced design of its many systems, the planet itself possesses no geologically ballooning capacities allowing it to expand its territory and resources indefinitely in order to accommodate the needs of ballooning human population growth and resource demand, new thinking must replace the shibboleths of limitless growth, at any cost, and "progress," a notion that enshrines often unsustainable technological advancement. It comes as no surprise that both supply Capitalism's supporting pillars. New economic arrangements need to replace the current dysfunctional model, which leads to:

Re-Defining Power and Success

As long as power and individual success imply competition, the structures of hierarchy must be maintained; but an alternate view might ascribe power to those creative, life-affirming forces in the world as opposed to human might, and success measured in terms of the degree to which a community looks after all its members, particularly the bearers of its artistic culture, its poets, and its most vulnerable.

These are some of the Who, What, Where and Hows by which we might begin to map a new existence, fracturing the West's linguistic barriers and creating the new, re-imagined world required if we are to outlive civilization. The question remains: If not now, when? And will we have sufficient time for When?

41. Tshxum

There will come a time perhaps not too far off when the San or Ju/wasi will have lost their history. In the words of Elizabeth Marshall Thomas,

> To live in the old way is to live with the sky. On the flat savannah, the sky is the spectacle, always with you, telling you where you are heading, how much more darkness or daylight you can expect, and what will happen next in terms of heat or cold, wind, or rain. All living things are alert for its signals. If the Ju/wasi knew the things of the earth for their qualities and their details, they knew the things of the sky for their power, their mystery, and their enormity and, as was true of the rest of their knowledge, they had known these things for a very long time.

According to Thomas, the Ju/wasi observed the constellations in much the same way as the so-called "civilized" world. Stories of Orion matched those of more familiar narratives in some respects, but there was one constellation that the San alone could identify, and whose brief turn in the sky presages the rainy season. One night, an old stargazer named Gau, who had been instructing Thomas' mother about the heavens, ran to her tent, awakening her well before dawn to show her, deep against the northeastern horizon, a star he called Tshxum, the Green Leaf Horn, identified by Thomas as Capella. She quotes her mother,

> For a moment of breathtaking beauty, in a seeming arc soaring over the sunrise glow, Capella and Canopus were paired, matched in brilliance and color, marking the north and south. An arc drawn between them would bracket the earth. With the Pleiades they formed a great embracing triangle.

But of all the earth's people only the Ju/wasi can actually detect this constellation *because the sky has shifted slightly since their historic memory began sometime in the Paleolithic, some 60,000 years ago.* That remarkable fact marks how old and unique the Ju/wasi are as a people.

But the time will come when the Ju/wasi will no longer recognize Tshxum in the night skies. And on the blackboard of our own nights strange figures will appear. What will they tell those who come eons after we are gone? Will they bear witness to our hubris? To the gods of our science that presumed to know everything while taking nothing from the wisdom of those who husbanded the landscape, giving and taking what they had to share with it in mutual agreement? Will we leave behind us warnings other than pitiful Barbie-doll figures of naked Caucasian male and female bodies etched on spacecraft and set adrift in the limitless expanse of space? Where will life, new life, begin? Will it elaborate itself from the strange white substance even now spreading on the floors of the ruptured reactors at Fukushima? What will it consist of? Will it answer to its own intelligence? Will it become a better keeper of the planet than we were? or will it multiply as mindlessly as we did?

42. Apologizing to a Whale

No scientist has ever observed whales coupling.

—Katy Payne

When friends ask me from time to time what I'm writing now, I tell them I feel impelled to apologize to a whale, but I feel bound to admit that what I took at first for the image of a living whale, endowed with mouth and seeing eye, turned out to be that of an even more gigantic piece of ice tossed up by the arctic melt. No matter. I tell them I am still considering the question: how to apologize to a whale for the planetary destruction caused by human agency, apologize, not in the sense of asking forgiveness, or even in the sense of trying to explain, or offering excuses, but as an act of acknowledgement to a being whose intelligence far exceeds my own, and as a small act of reverence to it and perhaps by extension to all living things great and small whose habitats are now in peril on this Earth.

When I share my project with a friend, I catch the gleam in his eye. "You want to hear a *real* whale story?"

Some years ago, long before whale watching became a consumer sport, friends of his built a concrete boat. They named her the *Stone Witch*. To launch her, they sailed her through the Golden Gate, heading south for Monterey, hoping to spot whales along the way. But barely past the Gate, fierce tides and wind—and seasickness—overtook them and forced them back to port.

Next voyage they reversed course, hugging the coast, sailing north from Monterey. This time, imagining that if there were to be any sightings along the way they would have to be in the far distance, my friend equipped himself with an arm-long telephoto lens. Still no whales were sighted until nearly in view of the Golden Gate, quite suddenly two whales surfaced, swimming as one, clasped in sexual embrace, all the while spiraling through the water to allow each 50-foot long partner to draw breath.

In their excitement the crew hung overboard. Some climbed the rigging. My friend straddled the main mast, thirty feet above the swell, straining for a longer shot, but the whales stuck to portside, swimming not ten feet from the Witch's flank.

Later, in the stillness of the dark room, he waited for the images to swim up at him through the hypos. Damn whales! He discovered all he'd captured was their eyes.

To this day he's still not certain what he sees in them. Is it ecstasy?

Do they mean to tell him something?

BIBLIOGRAPHY

BOOKS:

Abley, Mark. *Spoken Here: Travels among Threatened Languages*. New York: Houghton Mifflin, 2003.

Anthony, David W. *The Horse, The Wheel And Language: How Bronze-Age Riders From The Eurasian Steppes Shaped The Modern World*. Princeton: Princeton University Press, 2007.

Anthony, Lawrence. *The Elephant Whisperer*. New York: St. Martin's Press, 2009.

———. *The Last Rhino*. New York: St. Martin's Press, 2012.

Ashcroft, Bill, Gareth Griffiths, and Helen Tiffin. *The Empire Writes Back*. New York: Routledge, 2003.

Bernal, Martin. *Black Athena*. New Brunswick: Rutgers University Press. 1987.

Bertell, Rosalie. *Planet Earth: The Latest Weapon of War*. Montréal: Black Rose Books, 2001.

Brisendine, Louann. *The Female Brain*. New York: Broadway Books, 2007.

———. *The Male Brain*. New York: Crown, 2010.

Carter, Forrest. *The Education of Little Tree*. Albuquerque: University of New Mexico Press, 1976.

Chapman, Marina. *The Girl With No Name*. New York: Pegasus. 2013.

Dalrymple, William. *Nine Lives: In Search of the Sacred in Modern India*. London: Bloomsbury. 2009.

Diamond, Jared. *Collapse: How Societies Choose to Fail or Succeed*. New York: Viking, 2005.

———. *The World Until Yesterday: What We Can Learn From Traditional Societies*. New York: Viking, 2012.

Edmeades, Baz. *Megafauna*. http:www.megafauna.com.

Ehret, Christopher. *History and the Testimony of Language*. Berkeley: University of California Press, 2010.

Eisler, Riane. *The Chalice and the Blade*. New York: Harper & Row, 1987.

Fanon, Franz. *The Wretched of the Earth*. New York: Grove Press, 1963.

Fell, Barry. *America B.C.: Ancient Settlers of the New World*. New York: Quadrangle/New York Times, 1975.

Fine, Cordelia. *Delusions of Gender*. New York: W.W. Norton & Company, 2010.

Flannery, Tim. *Eternal Frontier: An Ecological History of North America and Its Peoples*. New York: Atlantic Monthly Press, 2001.

Forbes, Jack D. *Columbus and Other Cannibals*. Brooklyn: Autonomedia, 1992.

Foucault, Michel. *Society Must Be Defended*. New York: Picador, 2003.

Gibson, Graeme. *Bedside Book of Beasts*. New York: Knopf-Doubleday, 2009.

Gilligan, Carol. *In a Different Voice*. Cambridge: Harvard University Press. 1982.

Gimbutas, Marija. *The Civilization of the Goddess*. New York: Harper Collins, 1991.

———. *The Goddesses and Gods of Old Europe*. Berkeley: U. C. Press, 1982.

———. *The Language of the Goddess*. New York: Harper & Row, 1989.

Gore, Al. *Earth in the Balance: Ecology and the Human Spirit*. New York: Plume/Penguin, 1993.

Graves, Robert. *The Greek Myths, Vol. 2*. Baltimore: Penguin Books, 1955.

Greenberg, Joel. *A Feathered River Across the Sky*. New York: Bloomsbury, 2014.

Greenberg, Joseph H. *Language in the Americas*. Stanford: Stanford University Press, 1987.

Haddock, Doris (Granny D). *Walking Across America in My 90th Year*. New York: Villard-Random House, 2001.

Halperin, Mark, and John Heilemann. *Double Down: Game Change*. New York: The Penguin Press, 2013.

Hawken, Paul. *Blessed Unrest. How the Longest Social Movement in History Is Restoring Grace, Justice, and Beauty to the World.* New York: Penguin, 2007.

Hedges, Chris. *Empire of Illusion: The End of Literacy and the Triumph of Spectacle.* New York: Nation Books, 2009.

Henderson, Hazel. *The Politics of the Solar Age: Alternatives to Economics.* Indianapolis: Knowledge Systems, Inc., 1988.

Hinton, Leanne. *Flutes of Fire: Essays on California Indian Languages.* Berkeley: Heyday, 1993.

Irigaray, Luce. *Ce sexe qui n'en est pas un.* Paris: Editions de Minuit, 1977.

———. *Sexes et genres à travers les langues: éléments de communication sexuée, français, anglais.* Paris: Grasset, 1990.

Jensen, Derrick, ed. *How Shall I Live My Life? On Liberating the Earth from Civilization.* Oakland: PM Press, 2008.

Kosol, Jonathan. *Rachel and Her Children.* New York: Crown, 1988.

Lovelock, James. *Gaia: A New Look at Life on Earth.* Oxford: Oxford University Press, 1995.

MacNeilage, Peter F. *The Origin of Speech.* Oxford: Oxford University Press, 2008.

Margulis, Lynn, and Dorion Sagan. *Microcosmos.* Berkeley: University of California Press, 1997.

McIntyre, Joan, ed. *Mind in the Waters.* New York: Project Jonah/Scribners/Sierra Club, 1974.

Melville, Herman. *Moby-Dick; or, The Whale.* New York: Harper & Bros., 1851.

Merchant, Carolyn. *The Death of Nature.* New York: Harper & Row, 1989.

Mouchot, Augustin. *La Chaleur solaire et ses applications industrielles.* See https://archive.org/details/lachaleursolair00moucgoog.

Mowat, Farley. *Never Cry Wolf.* New York: Bantam, 1979.

Nolman, Jim. *The Charged Border.* New York: Henry Holt & Co., 1999.

Nye, Andrea, ed. *Philosophy of Language: The Big Questions.* Hoboken: Wiley-Blackwell, 1998.

Propp, Vladimir. Ja. Translated by Lise Gruel-Apert. *Les Racines historiques du conte merveilleux.* Paris: Gallimard, 1983.

Relethford, John H. *Fundamentals of Biological Anthropology.* Mountain View: Mayfield Publishing Co., 1994.

Renfrew, Colin, and Paul Bahn. *Archeology: Theories, Methods and Practice.* New York: Thames & Hudson, 1991.

Rimbaud, Arthur, tr. Mathieu, Bertrand. *A Season in Hell & Illuminations.* Brockport, NY: BOA Editions, Ltd., 1991.

Scheer, Hermann. *Energy Autonomy.* Translated by Jeremiah M. Reimer. Sterling, Va.: Earthscan, 2007.

Sheldrake, Rupert. *Dogs That Know When Their Owners Are Coming Home And Other Unexplained Powers Of Animals.* New York: Crown, 1999.

———. *The Presence of the Past.* New York: Crown, 1999.

Shlain, Leonard. *The Alphabet vs. the Goddess: The Conflict Between Word And Image.* New York: Viking, 1999.

———. *Sex, Time and Power: How Women's Sexuality Shaped Human Evolution.* New York: Penguin, 2003.

Silver, Shirley, and Wick R. Miller. *American Indian Languages: Cultural and Social Contexts.* Tucson: The University of Arizona Press. 1997.

Slater, Phillip. *A Dream Deferred.* Boston: Beacon Press, 1991.

———. *The Pursuit of Loneliness.* Boston: Beacon Press. 1970.

Tainter, Joseph. *Collapse of Complex Societies.* New York: Cambridge University Press, 1988.

Taussig, Michael. *Shamanism, Colonialism and the Wild Man.* Chicago: The University of Chicago Press, 1987.

Thomas, Elizabeth Marshall. *The Old Way.* New York: Farrar Straus, 2006.

Van der Post, Laurens. *The Lost World of the Kalahari.* New York: William Morrow & Company, 1958.

Wade, Nicholas. *Before the Dawn: Recovering the Lost History of Our Ancestors.* New York: Penguin, 2006.

Wakeford, Tom. *Liaisons of Life: From Hornworts to Hippos.* New York: Wiley, 2002.

Wells, Peter S. *How Ancient Europeans Saw the World: Visions, Patterns, and the Shaping of the Mind in Prehistoric Times.* Princeton: Princeton U. Press, 2012.

Whorf, Benjamin Lee. *Four Articles on Metalinguistics.* Washington, D.C.: Foreign Service Institute, Department of State, 1950.

———. *Language, Thought, and Reality.* Cambridge: The MIT Press, 1956.

Williams, Heather Andrea. *Help Me to Find My People.* Chapel Hill: University of North Carolina Press, 2012.

Wilson, E.O. *On Human Nature.* Cambridge: Harvard University Press, 1978.

Wright, Richard. *A Short History of Progress.* Toronto: House of Anansi, 2005.

ARTICLES:

Abdulghani, Samira, quoted in "Research links rise in Fallujah birth defects..." by Martin Chulov. *The Guardian,* 2010. http://www.theguardian.com/world/2010/dec/30/faulluja-birth-defects-iraq.

Achtenberg, Emily. "Earth First? Bolivia's Mother Earth Law Meets the Neo-Extractivist Economy." North American Congress on Latin America. November 16, 2012. https://nacla.org/blog/2012/11/16/earth-first-bolivia's-mother-earth-law-meets-neo-extractivist-economy.

Aviv, Rachel. "Netherland." *New Yorker,* December 10, 2012.

Barton, David. "Potentially Confusing & Embarrassing Differences between American and British English." http://iteslj.org/Articles/Barton-UK-USwords.html.

Beal, Tarcisio. "An Urgent Need: Example From the Top." *La Voz de la Esperanza,* May 2014.

Bosker, Bianca. "Clifford Nass on 'Seductive Tech and Why You Treat Your Phone Like a Friend.'" *Huffington Post,* March 3, 2003. http://www.huffingtonpost.com/2013/03/03/clifford-nass_n_2792780.html.

Buxton, Nick. "The Law of Mother Earth: Behind Bolivia's Historic Bill." Yes Magazine, April 21, 2011. http://www.yesmagazine.org/planet/

the-law-of-mother-earth-behind-bolivias-historic-bill.

Chossudovsky, Michel. "Ukraine's Gold Reserves Secretly Flown Out and Confiscated by the New York Federal Reserve?" http://www.global-research.ca/ukraines-gold-reserves-secretely-flown-out-and-confiscated-by-the-new-york-federal-reserve/5373446.

Chossudovsky, Michel. "The Globalization of Poverty: Deconstructing the New World Order." http://www.globalresearch.ca/the-globalization-of-poverty-deconstructing-the-new-world-order/29554.

Churchill, Ward. "History Not Taught is History Forgot: Columbus' Legacy of Genocide." (Excerpted from the book *Indians are Us* (Common Courage Press, 1993). http://www.mit.edu/~thistle/v9/9.11/1columbus.html.

Cohn, Carol. "Slick'ems, Glick'ems, Christmas Trees and Cookie Cutters: Nuclear Language and How We Learned to Pat the Bomb." *Bulletin of Atomic Scientists, Vol. 43 (1987), pp. 17–24.* See military language in informal speech: http://www.answers.com/topic/military-language-informal-speech#ixzz2o2VtJPjg.

Cortez, Marisol. "Beyond Development: Alternative, Models and Tactics." *Voz de la Esperanza*, July/August 2013, Vol. 26, Issue 6.

Delightmakers.com. "Wild Elephants Gather Inexplicably." http://delightmakers.com/news/wild-elephants-gather-inexplicably-mourn-death-of-elephant-whisperer.

Diné Water Rights. "A Long Historical Campaign of Genocide Against the Diné." http://dinewaterrights.org/a-long-historical-campaign-of-genocide-against-the-dineh.

Donnelly, Jon. "Lone Wolf: A Forsaken Predator Reappears." *Orion Magazine,* September/October, 2013.

Etelson, Erica. "Is Modern Technology Killing Us?" Truthout, September 19, 2014.

Garrigues, Lisa Gale. "Migrant Farmworkers Find Paths Out of Poverty Through Incubator Farms." Truthout, September 12, 2014.

Gorry, Conner. "Over the Hills & Far Away: Rural Health in Cuba." *MEDICC Review*, 2012. http://www.medicc.org/mediccreview/pdf.php?lang=&id=232.

Greenwald, Noah. "Death of Yellowstone's Most Famous Wolf Is a Troubling Sign of Things to Come." http://www.commondreams.org/view/2013/12/05-5.

GRITtv: "The Power of Co-Ops." http://www.truth-out.org/speakout/item/23384-the-power-of-co-ops, April 29, 2014.

Hallet, D. et al. "Aboriginal Language Knowledge and Youth Suicide." *Journal of Cognitive Development* #22, pp. 392-399, 2007.

Hedges, Chris. "The Crime of Peaceful Protest." ICH Newsletter, April 28, 2014. http://www.informationclearinghouse.info/article38359.htm.

Henderson, Hazel. "Peaceful Transitions From the Nuclear to the Solar Age," 2014. http://www.commondreams.org/views/2014/05/23/peaceful-transitions-nuclear-solar-age.

Hockett, Charles F. "The Origins of Language." *Scientific American*, 203: 89ff. September, 1960.

Horrigan, John. "The Night the Stars Fell." http://www.historylecture.org/starsfell.html.

House of Representatives. "Committee Democrats Release New Report Detailing Hydraulic Fracturing Products." http://democrats.energy-commerce.house.gov/index.php?q=news/committee-democrats-release-new-report-detailing-hydraulic-fracturing-products.

Jamail, Dahr. "Crop Growing – Open Source Farming." Truthout, August 10, 2014.

Jamie, Kathleen. "Shape Shifting: How Animal Art Made Us Human." *Orion Magazine*, September/October, 2013.

Jones, Adam. "Case Study: The European Witch Hunts, c. 1450-1750." http://www.gendercide.org/case_witchhunts.html.

Kaplan, Matt. "Elephants Recognize the Voices of Their Enemies." *Nature*, March 10, 2014. http://www.scientificamerican.com/article/elephants-recognize-the-voices-of-their-enemies/?WT.mc_id=send-to-friend.

Leslie, Jacques. "The Goddess Theory: Controversial UCLA Archeologist Marija Gimbutas Argues That the World Was at Peace When God Was a Woman." June 11, 1989. http://articles.latimes.com/1989-06-11/magazine/tm-2975_1_marija-gimbutas-gods-of-old-europe-indo-european/4.

Linzey, Thomas. "Of Corporations, Law, and Democracy: Claiming the Rights of Communities and nature." 2006. http://neweconomy.net/publications/lectures/of-corporations-law-and-democracy.

Livingston, Thomas. "La Bolivie d'Evo Morales va investir 2 milliards dans l'énergie nucléaire." L'enereek, October 7, 2014. http://lenergeek.com/2014/10/07/la-bolivie-devo-morales-va-investir-2-milliards-dans-lenergie-nucleaire.

Lundberg, Jan. Interviewed by Derrick Jensen in *How Shall I Live My Life*. http://www.culturechange.org/about_jan.htm.

Martone, Robert. "Scientists Discover Children's Cells Living in Mothers' Brains." *Scientific American,* December 4, 2012.

Norberg-Hodge, Helena. "The Multiple Benefits of Economic Localization." Truthout, September 20, 2014.

Orosco, Jose-Antonio. "Dr. King's Lesson for the Climate Justice Movement." http://www.commondreams.org/view/2014/01/06-2.

Pollan, Michael. "The Intelligent Plant." *The New Yorker,* December 23, 2013. http://www.newyorker.com/reporting/2013/12/23/131223fa_fact _pollan?printable=true&currentPage=all.

Ramares-Watson, Kellia. "A Book Review: *Devil's Tango: How I Learned the Fukushima Step by Step* by Cecile Pineda." http://www.leftistreview.com/2013/09/11/fukushima-step-by-step/kelliaramares/#sthash.bH-ClVcdS.dpuf.

Reed, Gail. "Cuba's Hurricane Preparedness: A Model for Florida and the Gulf Coast?" Institute for Public Policy. http://www.accuracy.org/release/cubas-hurricane-preparedness-a-model-for-florida-and-the-gulf-coast/ August 24, 2012.

Roberts, David. "There's a gender divide on nuclear power, but it doesn't mean what you think it means," *Vox: energy & environment*, May 27, 2015. http://www.vox.com/2015/5/27/8665401/nuclear-power-gender.

Robinson, Sara. "Why Patriarchal Men Are Utterly Petrified of Birth Control and Why We'll Still Be Fighting About It 100 Years From Now." http://www.alternet.org/story/154144/why_patriarchal_men_are_utterly_petrified_of_birth_control_--_and_why_we%27ll_still_be_fighting_about_it_100_years_from_now?akid=8270.34521.aRSTza&rd=1&t=8. 2014.

Rohrer, Finlo. "The Slow Death of Purposeless Walking." BBC News-magazine. http://www.bbc.com/news/magazine-27186709, May 1, 2014.

Rozoff, Rick. "Ukraine, Syria, Venezuela and Beyond: Beware the Wars of March." http://www.globalresearch.ca/ukraine-syria-venezuela-and-beyond-beware-the-wars-of-march/5373639.

Ruch, Peter. "Learning to Live in the Anthropocene." *Common Dreams,* November 22, 2013. http://www.commondreams.org/views/2013/11/22/learning-live-anthropocene.

Sacks, Oliver. "The Mental Life of Plants and Worms, Among Others." *New York Review of Books,* Vol. LXI, Number 7, April 24, 2014.

Sahlins, Marshall D. "The Origins of Society," *Scientific American.* 203: 62ff, September, 1960.

The Onion. "New Report Finds Climate Change Caused by 7 Billion Key Individuals." http://www.theonion.com/articles/new-report-finds-climate-change-caused-by-7-billio,34658/.

Thicke, Lori. "If a Tree Falls…" http://lorithicke.com/2014/04/28/suicide. 2014.

Wasserman, Harvey. "Let's Bury King C.O.N.G. (coil, oil, nukes, and natural gas) at People's Climate March." *Counterpunch*, September 12-14, 2014.

Wikipedia. "List of Bilderberg participants." http://en.wikipedia.org/wiki/List_of_Bilderberg_participants#Presidents.

———. "Law Of The Rights Of Mother Earth." http://en.wikipedia.org/wiki/Law_of_the_Rights_of_Mother_Earth.

World Conference on Climate Change and the Rights of Mother Earth. http://pwccc.wordpress.com/programa.

Zeese, Kevin and Flowers, Margaret. "Militarism and Violence are So Yesterday: It's Time to Make Peace the Reality." http://truth-out.org/opinion/item/20146-militarism-and-violence-are-so-yesterday-its-time-to-make-peace-the-reality.

FILM, VIDEO & AUDIO:

"A Fierce Green Fire." Dir. Mark Kitchell, 2013.

"The Alphabet and the Goddess." Lecture by Leonard Shlain at Pepperdine University. http://www.youtube.com/watch?v=2QQuD62RxrU.

"Bidder #70." Dirs. Beth and George Gage. 2010.

"Big Mountain Trilogy." TUC Radio http://www.tucradio.org/native.html.

"Black Fish." Dir. Gabriela Cowperthwaite, 2013.

"Chasing Ice." Dir. Jeff Orlowski, 2012.

"Community Rights Charters for Yukon." Margil, Mari. October 2, 2014. https://www.youtube.com/watch?v=RA3YGEJ8sJg.

"Forum." Michael Krasny interviews Lera Boroditsky. http://www.kqed.org/a/forum/R201202021000.

"Frozen Planet." Narrated by Sir David Attenborough. BBC, 2014.

"Happiness." Dir. Thomas Balmes. 2013.

"How Smart Are Animals?" PBS Nova: http://video.pbs.org/video/1777525840/.

"Instinct." Dir. Jon Turteltau; starring Anthony Hopkins and Cuba Gooding. Based on *My Ismael* by Daniel Quinn. 1999.

"In the Light of Reverence: Protecting America's Sacred Lands." Dir. Christopher McLeod. Sacred Land Film Project, Earth Island Institute, 2002.

"In Their Own Words." Kimon Kotos interviews Cecile Pineda on DSE-TV, Muskegon http://www.youtube.com/watch?v=KCDUUB46IPo&list=PL7g1LIVSXLKMVRGdS5MsWHUW5VbDOmahN&index=1.

"Islands of Sanctuary: Aboriginal Australians and Native Hawaiians reclaim land and resist the erosion of culture and the environment." Dir. Christopher McLeod. Sacred Land Film, Earth Island Institute, 2012.

Multilanguage Documentaries. "The Animal Communicator," Dir.,

Swati Thiyagarajan. January 28, 2015. https://www.youtube.com/watch?v=TfP-XBUbMvs.

"Oscar Olivera: The 'Water War' of Cochabamba and the Rights of Nature." Scheidler, Fabian. Kontext-TV, July 2, 2012. http://www.kontext-tv.de/broadcast/020712/water-crisis/oscar-olivera-cochabamba.

"Of Corporations, Law, and Democracy: Claiming the Rights of Communities and nature." Linzey, Thomas. 2006. http://neweconomy.net/publications/lectures/of-corporations-law-and-democracy.

"On Being," Kirsta Tippett interviews Katy Payne. http://www.onbeing.org/program/whale-songs-and-elepant-loves/particulars/346.

"Sacred Lands Film Project." Dir. Christopher McLeod. Bullfrog Films. 2014.

"Stefan Molyneux of Freedomain Radio interviews Lloyd deMause, the author of 'The Origins of War in Child Abuse.'" http://www.informa-tionclearinghouse.info/article37338.htm.

"The Stranger." Dir. Satyajit Ray. DD Productions, 1991.

"We Come As Friends." Dir. Hubert Sauper, Sauper/Kranselbinder Productions, 2013.

ANNOTATED BIBLIOGRAPHY (SELECTED)

Anthony, David. *The Horse, The Wheel And Language: How Bronze-Age Riders From The Eurasian Steppes Shaped The Modern World*. Princeton: Princeton University Press, 2007. A seminal examination of Kurgan culture mediated by the archeological pre-literate bibliography of its grave offerings. It supports assertions in section 24.

Anthony, Lawrence. *The Elephant Whisperer*. New York: St. Martin's Press, 2009.

————. *The Last Rhino*. New York: St. Martin's Press, 2012. Taken together, Anthony's accounts chronicle the trajectory of a remarkably astute self-trained naturalist over his many senior years as owner and director of a Zululand game reserve. It supports assertions in sections 16 and 17.

Bertell, Rosalie. *Planet Earth: The Latest Weapon of War*. Montréal: Black Rose Books, 2001. Bertell (1929-2012), mathematician and physicist by training and the author of the seminal work on the nuclear industry, *No Immediate Danger*, writes here about the harms done the planet by the contamination resulting from militarism and warfare. The text offers background support for suggestions in section 39.

Bose, Jagadish. Because he lived and worked as a Renaissance man, the trajectory of Bose's thought in multiple fields reflects his almost exploding range of interests. A full bibliography is indicated. Many useful articles are directly available on the internet at http://en.wikipedia.org/wiki/Jagadish_Chandra_Bose#Bibliography. (Note: Bose's work with plants informs section 36.)

Churchill, Ward. "History Not Taught is History Forgot: Columbus' Legacy of Genocide." (Excerpted from the book *Indians are Us* (Common Courage Press, 1994) http://www.mit.edu/~thistle/v9/9.11/1columbus.html. A central work on the oppression of Third World societies and people of color throughout human history, supported by horrifying numbers. The text supports statistics cited in "Triumphs of Western Civilization," section 29.

Edmeades, Baz. *Megafauna*. http:www.megafauna.com. Available on the internet, a key work on the trajectory of a history that kills everything that lives, starting with the low hanging fruit of the megafauna, such that with the exception of the buffalo, all these many species have vanished from the Earth. The last European wild bear met its death in Switzerland in 2013. The last auroch, ancestor of domestic cattle, met its death in the 18th century. This source supports Section 3.

Fanon, Franz. *The Wretched of the Earth*. New York: Grove Press, 2005. The seminal work on popular movements and revolution. Because its first chapter is seen as advocating violent overthrow, much of Fanon's wisdom tends to get overlooked. A good approach is to read *The Wretched of the Earth* backwards, foregrounding Fanon's infinite wisdom. This text underpins much of section 30.

Gimbutas, Marija. *The Civilization of the Goddess*. New York: Harper Collins, 1991. Taken together, the Gimbutas texts chronicle the prehistory of the civilization of Old Europe which existed for millennia prior to the Kurgan invasion of c. 3,500 B.C. They cover multiple ground: how people fed themselves; how they traded, sometimes over long distances; how they worshipped; how they governed themselves; and their social organization; all based on the actual pre-literate bibliography recorded in their grave offerings, which Gimbutas catalogues and illustrates in extensive detail. These sources inform sections 24 and 27.

———. *The Goddesses and Gods of Old Europe*. Berkeley: U. C. Press, 1982.

———. *The Language of the Goddess*. New York: Harper & Row, 1989.

Gore, Al. *Earth in the Balance*. New York: Penguin/Plume, 1993. Written some 40 years after Rachel Carson's work first appeared, this work, in its encyclopedic coverage not only of all Earth systems affected by global warming but human response to it, reads as a criminal indictment of all the world bodies which, in the intervening 25 years since its publication, have addressed global warming to such equivocating effect.

Greenberg, Joseph H. *The Languages of Africa* (2nd ed. with additions and corrections). Bloomington: Indiana University, 1966.

———. *Language in the Americas*. Stanford: Stanford University Press, 1987. Any discussion of comparative linguistics must rely on the extraordinary pre-electronic cataloguing mind of Joseph Greenberg. His research and radical re-identification and categorization of mankind's earliest languages, especially the three click languages collectively named Khoisan, are central to my work here and reinforced by new evidence based on mito-chondrial DNA. Greenberg's work on African Khoisan underpins the discussion in sections 11 and 20.)

Hawken, Paul. *Blessed Unrest: How the Longest Social Movement in History Is Restoring Grace, Justice, and Beauty to the World*. New York: Penguin.

2007. A compendium suggesting how the world's political landscape is characterized by the dialectic of resistance by millions of groups addressing the various issues of our discontent. Hawken's work informs many of the suggestions in section 39.

Hedges, Chris. *Empire of Illusion: The End of Literacy and the Triumph of Spectacle.* New York: Nation Books, 2009. A critical pulse-taking of the discontents of our present dystopia. Its section on pornography informs much of the discussion on political matters of gender and gender equality found in section 26.

Hinton, Leanne. *Flutes of Fire: Essays on California Indian Languages.* Berkeley: Heyday, 1993. A series of articles published by this now-emerita of the Department of Anthropology of the University of California at Berkeley whose work has centered on the cultures and languages of California's First Nations. Her work on Wintu underpins key points in sections 25 and 39.

Irigaray, Luce. *Ce sexe qui n'en est pas un.* Paris: Editions de Minuit, 1977.

—. *Sexes et genres à travers les langues: éléments de communication sexuée, français, anglais.* Paris: Grasset, 1990. No discussion of gender and gender equality is complete without examination of Irigaray's work. In the latter work cited here, she argues for the re-sexualization of language. It underpins the discussion in section 28.

Lovelock, James. *Gaia: A New Look at Life on Earth.* Oxford: Oxford University Press, 1995. The first to advance the Gaia hypothesis, an atmospheric chemist by formation, Lovelock's work is cited in section 36 in connection with Earth's aloof gases, suggesting that the planet's atmosphere is mediated by the collective activity of living microorganisms producing renewed amounts of the reactive gases necessary to support life on our planet. His work figures in Section 36.

Lundberg, Jan. Interviewed by Derrick Jensen in *How Shall I Live My Life? On Liberating the Earth from Civilization.* Oakland: PM Press, 2008. Lundberg's detailed discussion of the culture of the automobile informs section 39.

Margulis, Lynn, and Dorion Sagan. *Microcosmos.* Berkeley: University of California Press, 1997. Margulis' work on endosymbiosis submits Darwinism to a radical re-evaluation. Darwin's tree-of-life model underpinning early discussion of evolution derives from a quintessentially hierarchical Western worldview. *Margulis' work, by proposing a radically different evolutionary model, has huge implications for a revised worldview privileging collaboration over hierarchy.* Her work underpins section 36.

Mouchot, Augustin. *La Chaleur solaire et ses applications industrielles.* https://archive.org/details/lachaleursolair00moucgoog. One of innumerable out-of-copyright treasures to be found directly on the Internet. Mouchot is one of the very first to have imagined the sun as a source of industrial power. His discoveries inform section 22.

Mowat, Farley. *Never Cry Wolf.* New York: Bantam, 1979. The work of this naturalist observing wolves in the Keewatin Basin in the 50s offers a detailed accounting of human/animal interface, animal language, and *the high degree of civilization displayed by wolf society,* all the more placing their relentless extermination in tragic relief. His work with wolves informs the discussion in section 19.

Nolman, Jim. *The Charged Border.* New York: Henry Holt & Co., 1999. Nolman is a composer, conceptual artist, and environmental activist. This 1999 work chronicles animal-human interface with pseudo-orcas in the straights off Vancouver. It informs observations cited in section 13.

Payne, Katy. Interviewed by Kirsta Tippett. "On Being," http://www.onbeing.org/program/whale-songs-and-elephant-loves/particulars/346. Katy Payne styles herself an acoustic biologist. In her interviews/appearances, she offers unique insights into the language structures primarily of humpbacks. In section 14, much of her experience with elephants is cited.

Pollan, Michael. "The Intelligent Plant." *New Yorker,* December 23, 2013. http://www.newyorker.com/reporting/2013/12/23/131223fa_fact_pollan ?printable=true&currentPage=all. Pollan's work on plant life and plant "language" is the source of another stunning revelation in section 36.

Shlain, Leonard. *The Alphabet vs. the Goddess: The Conflict Between Word And Image.* New York: Viking, 1999. A keystone for the *Whale* project derives from Shlain's argument that, generally speaking, for each step of the evolutionary ladder, something from previous existence tends to get left behind. It informs and underpins the discussion in section 8 and some subsequent sections.

Shlain, Leonard. *Sex, Time and Power: How Women's Sexuality Shaped Human Evolution.* New York: Penguin, 2003. Some of Shlain's discussion of misogyny is included in section 27.

Slater, Phillip. *A Dream Deferred.* Boston: Beacon Press, 1991. Taken together, these texts show Slater to be one of the most important voices mapping the landscape of our political and societal discontents. Seminal to *Whale*, his work informs much of the political tenor of the work. Its perceptions underpin many of the topics in Section 39.

―――. *The Pursuit of Loneliness.* Boston: Beacon Press. 1970.

Thomas, Elizabeth Marshall. *The Old Way.* New York: Farrar Straus, & Giroux, 2006. Because Elizabeth Marshall Thomas grew up with the Nyae-nyae group of the Ju/'hoansi, her report of their tribal status in the present day is all the more reliable. Her account underpins one of the most *startling revelations* of *Whale,* namely that the historic memory of the Ju/'hoansi goes back so far, it allows them still to access astronomical time/space circa 60,000 B.C.! Her work underpins sections 20 and 40.

Van der Post, Laurens. *The Lost World of the Kalahari.* New York: William Morrow & Company, 1958. One of the first ethnologies describing the original, tribal way of life of the Ju/'hoansi (commonly called the San, inhabitants of the Kalahari Desert). Van der Post was not an ethnographer by training, but the last sixty or so pages of his account of a 1950s expedition into the Kalahari offers a fleshed out description of many of the aspects (excepting language) of the original, traditional way of life of these deeply civilized people. This report underpins section 20.

Wade, Nicholas. *Before the Dawn: Recovering the Lost History of Our Ancestors.* New York: Penguin, 2006. Recently published, Wade's text supplies the essential bridge between Greenberg's identification and classification of Khoisan with recent discoveries drawing on mitochondrial DNA. His work underpins section 26 and offers irrefutable corroboration of Greenberg's work.

Whorf, Benjamin Lee. *Language, Thought, and Reality.* Cambridge: The MIT Press, 1956. A slim volume of articles, the one and only offering by Whorf, who all his life worked as a chemist for the Hartford Fire Insurance Company. An almost exclusively autodidact linguist, his work with First Nations languages, primarily Hopi, offers an invaluable window into the ontology of a people whose language presents a stunning contrast to Western European thought as embedded in Kurgan Proto-Indo-European-derived languages. His work underpins the discussion in section 25 and the substantive suggestions in section 39.

Zeese, Kevin and Margaret Flowers. "Militarism and Violence are So Yesterday: It's Time to Make Peace the Reality." http://truth-out.org/opinion/item/20146-militarism-and-violence-are-so-yesterday-its-time-to-make-peace-the-reality. A seminal article which provides the launching pad for the conclusions reached in section 39.

ACKNOWLEDGMENTS

I am grateful to all who helped me remember the gifts of the Earth and consider the intransigence of the human race: Alan Bonny, Ignacio Chapela, David Leneman, Michael Leneman, Joanna Macy, Michelle Phillipot, Donald Goldmacher, Sheila Goldmacher, Raymond Lee Davis, Jiwon Chong, Susan Harman, Louise Dunlap, Megan Rice, Ruthie Sackheim, Mark Kitchell, Alice Slater, Leslie Curchack, Bob Gorringe, Paul Kangas, Maria Gilardin, Katherine Davis, Webb Mealy, Umi Hagitani, Jonathan Pool, Srinivas Reddy, Skaidrite Rubene, Kay Cumbow, Bonnie Urfer, Barbara George, Roger Herreid, Lauren Elder, Jackie Cabasso, Susan Quinlan, Siri Mangerin, Mylee Casperson, René Scofield, Margaret Shapiro, Andrea Snow, Hale Thatcher, Sandra Alcosser, Sydney Carson, Ruth Lynn Craig, Marlene Schoofs, Hattie Nestel, Marcia Gagliardi, Sheila Parks, the late Rhoda Curtis, Carol Urner, Kimon Kotos, Nick Thabit, Phoebe Sorgen, Jane Miller, and Francisco Lomelí, and my long-suffering publisher, Bryce Milligan of Wings Press. I thank Tara Hands who wired flowers to a whale; Sonia Allison who lent me a poem; Andrey Timokhin, who acquainted me with astronomy; Josh Marker, and Michael Houser who acquainted me with linguistics; my students at San Diego State; the members of my company, Theatre of Man; my sangha members; the anti-nuclear activists who joined me in 2011 to dance the *Devil's Tango*; all who shared with me my curiosity about languages and human migrations, beginning with my father; and all whose love of the planet's glory inspired me, beginning with my mother; and my grandmother, Cecile, who witnessed the Perseid Shower of 1866 and put up with my grandfather.

AUTHOR'S NOTE

For most of my life, I have assumed that somehow I am the little guy with the broom and dust pan bringing up the rear behind the elephants and the other heavy lifters.

My politics originate with the Dominican nuns who taught me during my grammar school years at Corpus Christi experimental parochial school in New York City. Illustrious graduates include both my contemporaries, the comedian George Carlin and Sister Megan Rice (age 84), who faced a 30-year sentence for cutting through four security perimeters protesting nuclear weapons of mass destruction at Y12 in Oakridge, Tennessee. She served three years in a detention center described by the *Daily News* as a hellhole before her case was finally dismissed. I became radicalized in 1969-1970 at San Francisco State University during the longest student strike in U.S. history. There I directed an agitprop student theater that aimed to shut down not only San Francisco State, but the entire state college system. That, in turn with my collaboration with the San Francisco Mime Troupe, led in some myserious way to founding and directing an experimental theater company, Theatre of Man, for twelve years, 1969-1981.

Since my graduate days, I have actively opposed the Vietnam War; U.S. interventions in Central America; and the preemptive attacks on Afghanistan and on Iraq, known as Gulf One, and Gulf Two. I participated with my affinity group, The Mourning Mothers, building seven nine-foot-tall puppets representing Iraqi women, their dead children cradled in their arms. We participated in demonstrations opposing the invasion of Iraq, both before March 19, and in many anti-war demonstrations since. I have participated in the 9/11 truth movement. I volunteered in the draft resistance movement in Oakland, California. I volunteered for the Black Panther Party's after-school tutoring program. I have addressed the S.F. Occupy Environmental Forum twice on the subject of the nuclear industry. I have demonstrated with Code Pink, World Can't Wait, ANSWER, Fukushima Response, No Nukes Action Committee, and am an active member of Nuclear Free California.

Besides the active participation cited above, following the events of 9/11 I have predominantly redirected my energies to publishing non-fiction because—given the extreme right shift in the political landscape—my perception is that the writing of fiction is an indulgence, which the times no longer allow.

Starting in 2005 with Katrina, with the ad hoc help I extended to its victims, and my later volunteer work with them, I was privileged to be allowed to record oral histories of the lives of some of the people I helped. This, in turn, led quite naturally to a play, *Like Snow Melting in Water*, where I was able to parlay the multiple voices of my Katrina respondents into a polyvocal tone poem, giving voice to the lives of elders stranded in a dying Japanese village who are forced to sell their land to the only bidder to come forward: a toxic waste disposal company. Based on a true story, the play was completed in 2008 and has had productions in Thailand and India.

My new trajectory quite naturally evolved into reportage. In 2009, I travelled to New Jersey, where over a ten-day period I interviewed Jean Blum, an Immigration Detention activist who, impelled by her memories of the Holocaust, founded a volunteer organization, ALAFFA, committed to working in the Patterson municipal prison where she was able to document conditions there, and lend vital assistance to some of its immigrant prisoners. She was the first to blow the whistle, alerting the Department of Homeland Security to the actual "disappearance" of an incarcerated Pakistani taxi driver. Ultimately, through her disclosure, the deaths of 106 more persons who died mysteriously in Immigrant Detention, many of them by "asphyxiation," were exposed by *The New York Times*. She shared her archive of primary sources with me. This led to a four-part feature article, "Finger in Goliath's Eye," published in La Bloga in 2010.

The week prior to the catastrophe still unfolding in Fukushima, a dying friend made an improbable request: "Write the Book of Life and Death." With the three explosions and meltdowns at Fukushima, I foresaw the potential for planetary destruction and the world-over contamination of soils, air, and water, as well as the food chain. Researched and written in white heat over a nine-month period, *Devil's Tango: How I learned the Fukushima Step by Step* appeared on the one-year anniversary of the disaster. Its reportage still remains topical today, three years after it first appeared. I followed its publication with regional and national touring from 2012 to the present, addressing the perils of the nuclear industry and urging the shift to sustainable alternatives to replace fossil and nuclear fuels.

When not involved in a long-term project, I blog at "Devil's Tango" from time to time. Some recent subjects include Ferguson: the question of hope; the arrest of a polar bear by the New York Police Department; the militarization and training by Israel Defense Forces of domestic American law enforcement in urban warfare; recent destabilization of the Ukraine and its connection to the looming global currency crisis; the repeated and predictable knee-jerk military reactions of an administration driven by the if-you-are-a-hammer-everything-looks-like-a-nail approach; and the affectless language bastardized by presidents and other public figures, which enables pathological lying as their daily practice.

Over the course of now nearly one hundred public appearances, I felt impelled by the perplexity voiced by many of my interlocutors about what *Apology to a Whale* calls "The Thing Without a Name." Informed by my study of archeology and comparative linguistics, I initiated what turned into my most compelling project to date. The writing of *Apology to a Whale* has occupied the past two years of my life. Besides archeology and linguistics, it has drawn on such other disciplines as animal behavior studies, natural history, botany, sociology, environmentalism, anthropology, women's studies, and contemporary politics. In many ways it has offered me an intensive program of postgraduate study because much of the scientific knowledge it draws upon had yet to be discovered during the course of my early academic career.

I am working now to insure that *Apology to a Whale* meets the readership it is meant to reach.

ABOUT THE AUTHOR

Cecile Pineda was born in Harlem, the daughter of a Mexican professor of Romance languages, and a Swiss-French mother. Her language of origin is French.

After some twelve years of producing and directing her own experimental theater company, Pineda began to write fiction. Her novels have been critically acclaimed, with *Face* winning the Commonwealth Club of California Gold Medal—a record for first fiction, the Sue Kaufman Prize, a National Book Award Nomination and a nomination for the 2014 Neustadt Prize. Her picaresque novel, *The Love Queen of the Amazon*, written with a NEA Fiction Fellowship, was named a Notable Book of the Year by *The New York Times*. Other novels include *Frieze*, set in 9th century India and Java; *Fishlight*, a fictional memoir of childhood; and two mononovels, *Bardo99*, in which the 20th century passes through a bardo state, and *Redoubt*, a meditation on gender. Her play, *Like Snow Melting in Water*, set in contemporary agrarian Japan, centers on themes of displacement and ecological collapse. It has had productions in India and Thailand in 2012 and 2013.

With *Three Tides*, a three-part memoir, oral history, and stage play to appear in the near future, Pineda shares with readers and writers-in-development her own creative process.

Pineda has been a peace activist from early life. More recently, she has turned her attention to issues affecting the sustainability of the planet. Published in 2012, *Devil's Tango: How I Learned the Fukushima Step by Step* is her anguished dissection of the nuclear industry seen through the lens of the industrial and planetary disaster still unfolding at Fukushima Daiichi.

Apology to a Whale is Pineda's second work of non-fiction. Adhering to the form she pioneered in *Devil's Tango*, the book reflects her growing awareness of the interconnectedness of all things on Earth, and the relationship between gender and economic injustice and ecological collapse. It is her apology to all living things for the destruction caused by the most abusive species on Earth. (And it's not the chimpanzees—they only come in second.)

Visit her website at cecilepineda.com

ABOUT BARBARA GEORGE (1948 – 2013)

Barbara George, née Epmeier, to whom this work is dedicated, was a committed artist and non-stop, lifetime environmentalist. A force unto herself, with her charm, wit, energy, and graciousness, she played an important role in major anti-nuclear campaigns from 1980 through the long campaign to close California's San Onofre reactor located on one of California's major faults. Following her graduation from Stanford University (where she appeared in 1970 with Pineda in a full production of the four Cuchulain Cycle plays by Yeats), she toured the country for several years, performing her one-woman show "Everything I Ever Wanted To Ask About Nukes And Was Afraid To Know." For years she lived in New York City, returning to California to become an Intervener at the CPUC hearings and to found Women's Energy Matters (WEM), which lobbied for renewable energy standards and energy efficiency. She played a critical part in the creation of Marin Clean Energy, a project of the Marin Energy Authority, which has become a national model, delivering clean energy to hundreds of thousands of Californian ratepayers every year. Not long before her death, she was a living, breathing part of the conversation at lunch when we listened rapt to the *real* whale story told by our friend and fellow activist, Roger Herreid.

For more information about Barbara, visit
http://vimeo.com/91388143

Colophon

This first edition of *Apology to a Whale: Words to Mend a World* by Cecile Pineda, has been printed on 55 pound EB Natural paper, containing a percentage of recycled fiber. Titles have been set in Aquiline Two and Onyx type, the text in Adobe Caslon type. All Wings Press books are designed and produced by Bryce Milligan.

On-line catalogue and ordering:
www.wingspress.com

Wings Press titles are distributed
to the trade by the
Independent Publishers Group
www.ipgbook.com
and in Europe by
www.gazellebookservices.co.uk

Also available as an ebook.